SEEN™

True Stories of
Marginalized Trailblazers

Rachel Carson

Birdie Willis • Rii Abrego
Kieran Quigley

Published by

BOOM! BOX™

Ross Richie CEO & Founder
Joy Huffman CFO
Matt Gagnon Editor-in-Chief
Filip Sablik President, Publishing & Marketing
Stephen Christy President, Development
Lance Kreiter Vice President, Licensing & Merchandising
Arune Singh Vice President, Marketing
Bryce Carlson Vice President, Editorial & Creative Strategy
Kate Henning Director, Operations
Spencer Simpson Director, Sales
Scott Newman Manager, Production Design
Elyse Strandberg Manager, Finance
Sierra Hahn Executive Editor
Jeanine Schaefer Executive Editor
Dafna Pleban Senior Editor
Shannon Watters Senior Editor
Eric Harburn Senior Editor
Sophie Philips-Roberts Associate Editor
Amanda LaFranco Associate Editor
Jonathan Manning Associate Editor
Gavin Gronenthal Assistant Editor
Gwen Waller Assistant Editor
Allyson Gronowitz Assistant Editor
Ramiro Portnoy Assistant Editor
Kenzie Rzonca Assistant Editor
Shelby Netschke Editorial Assistant
Michelle Ankley Design Coordinator
Marie Krupina Production Designer
Grace Park Production Designer
Chelsea Roberts Production Designer
Samantha Knapp Production Design Assistant
José Meza Live Events Lead
Stephanie Hocutt Digital Marketing Lead
Esther Kim Marketing Coordinator
Breanna Sarpy Live Events Coordinator
Amanda Lawson Marketing Assistant
Holly Aitchison Digital Sales Coordinator
Morgan Perry Retail Sales Coordinator
Megan Christopher Operations Coordinator
Rodrigo Hernandez Operations Coordinator
Zipporah Smith Operations Assistant
Jason Lee Senior Accountant
Sabrina Lesin Accounting Assistant

BOOM! BOX

BOOM! Studios, 5670 Wilshire Boulevard, Suite 400, Los Angeles, CA 90036-5679. Printed in China. First Printing.

ISBN: 978-1-68415-648-1, eISBN: 978-1-64668-047-4

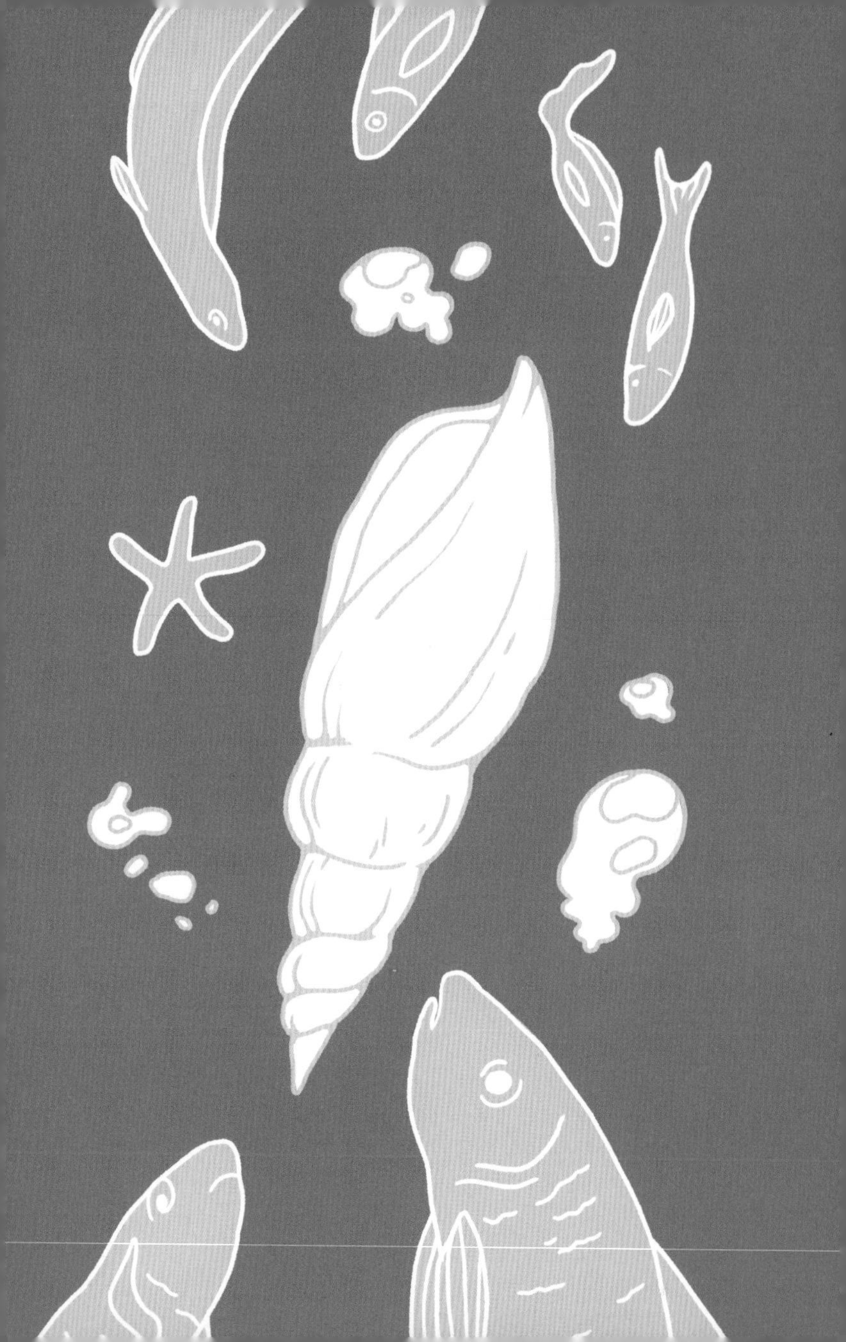

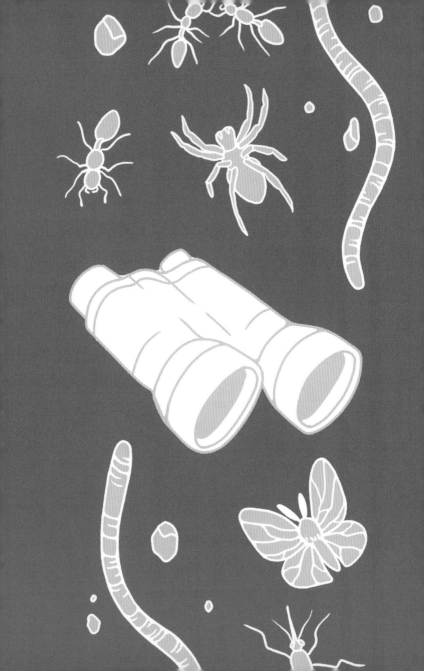

SEEN™

—Rachel Carson—

Written by **BIRDIE WILLIS**
Illustrated by **RII ABREGO**
Colored by **KIERAN QUIGLEY**
Lettered by **DC HOPKINS**

Cover by **RII ABREGO**

Designer **MARIE KRUPINA**
Assistant Editor **KENZIE RZONCA**
Editor **SHANNON WATTERS**

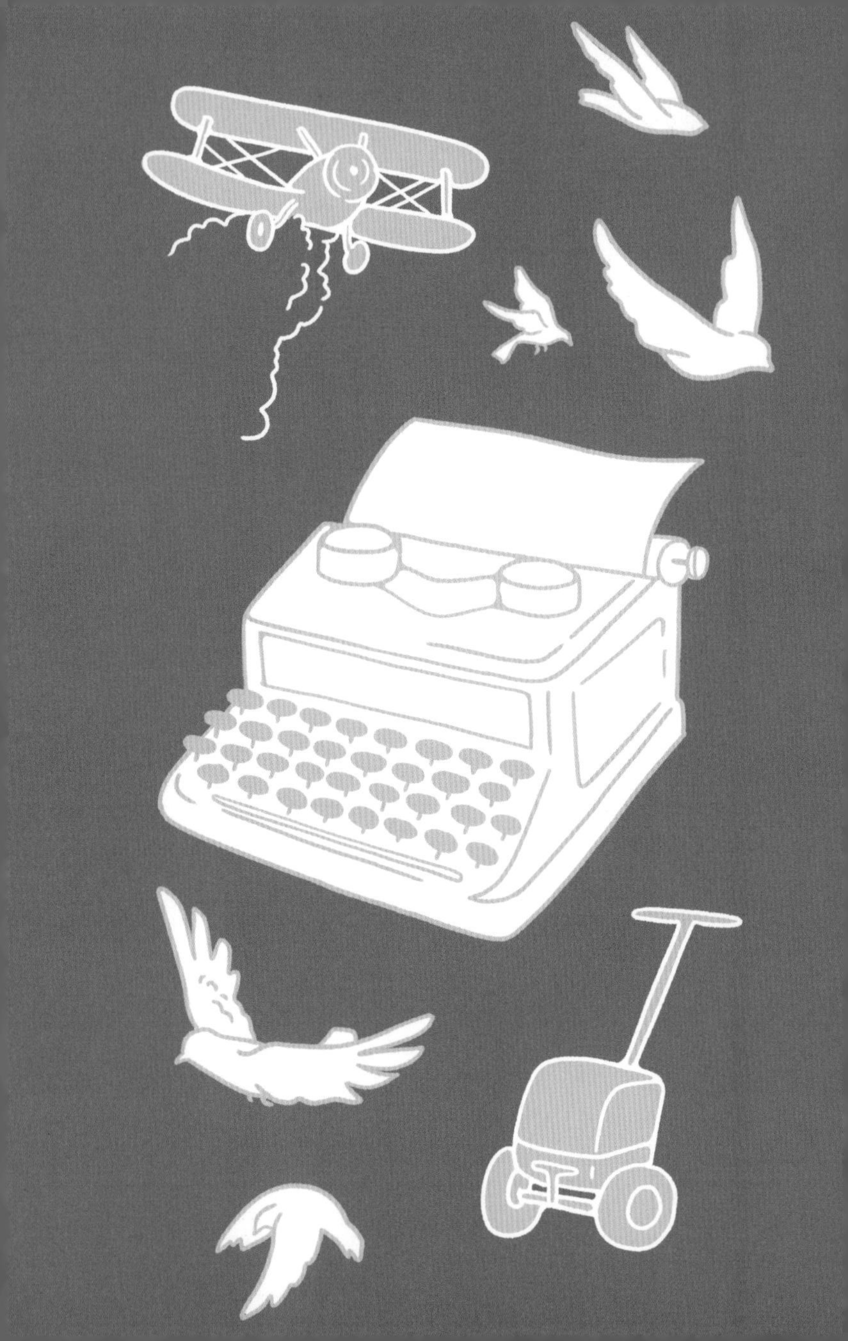

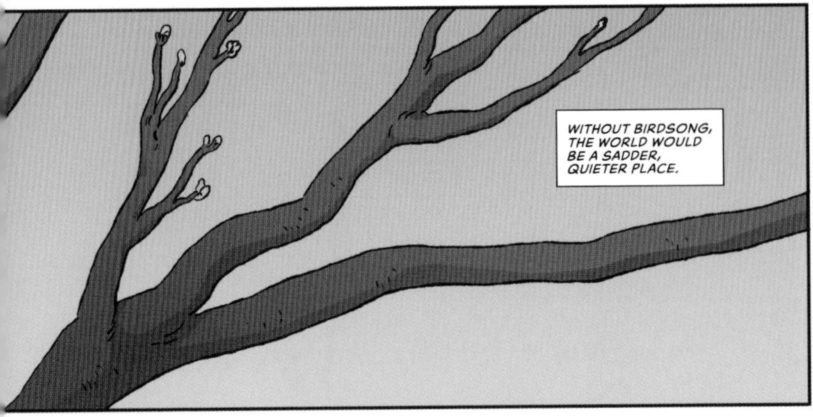
WITHOUT BIRDSONG, THE WORLD WOULD BE A SADDER, QUIETER PLACE.

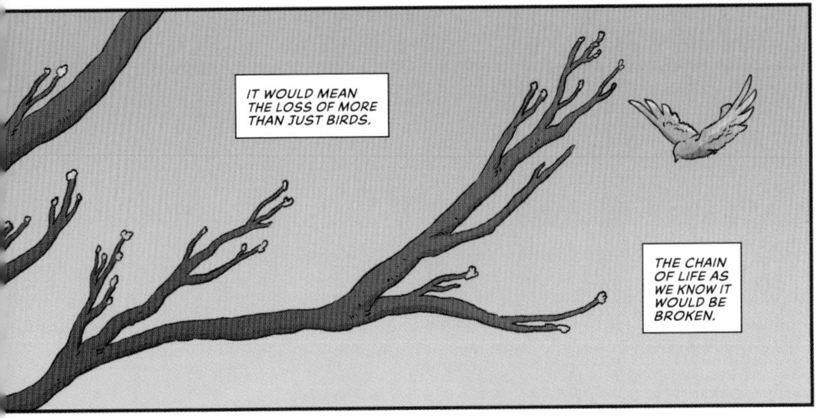
IT WOULD MEAN THE LOSS OF MORE THAN JUST BIRDS.
THE CHAIN OF LIFE AS WE KNOW IT WOULD BE BROKEN.

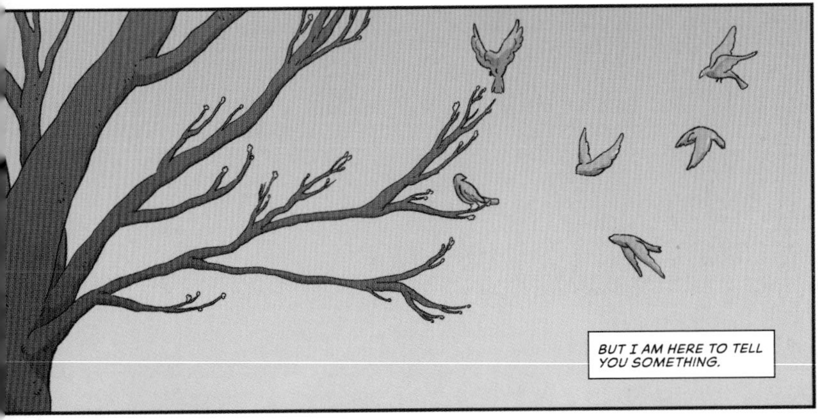
BUT I AM HERE TO TELL YOU SOMETHING.

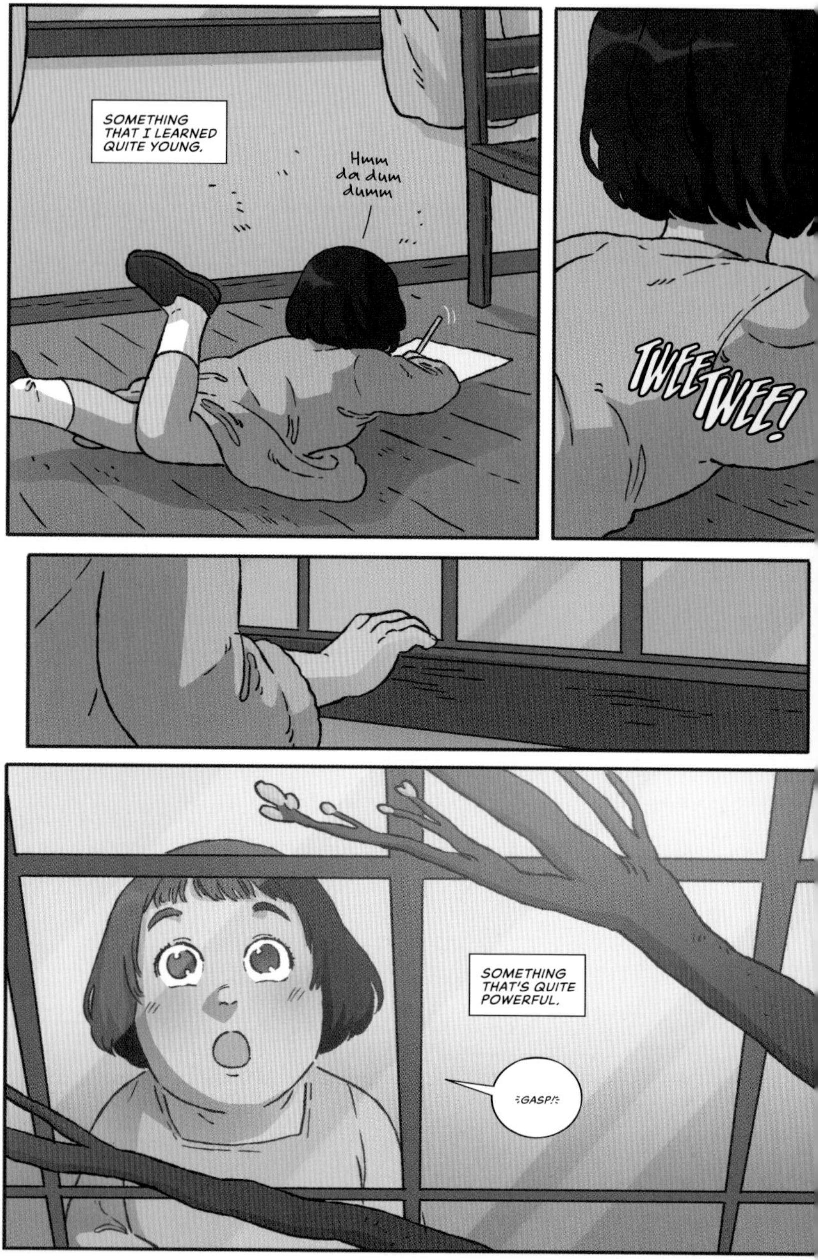
SOMETHING THAT I LEARNED QUITE YOUNG.
Hmm da dum dumm
TWEE TWEE!
SOMETHING THAT'S QUITE POWERFUL.
GASP!

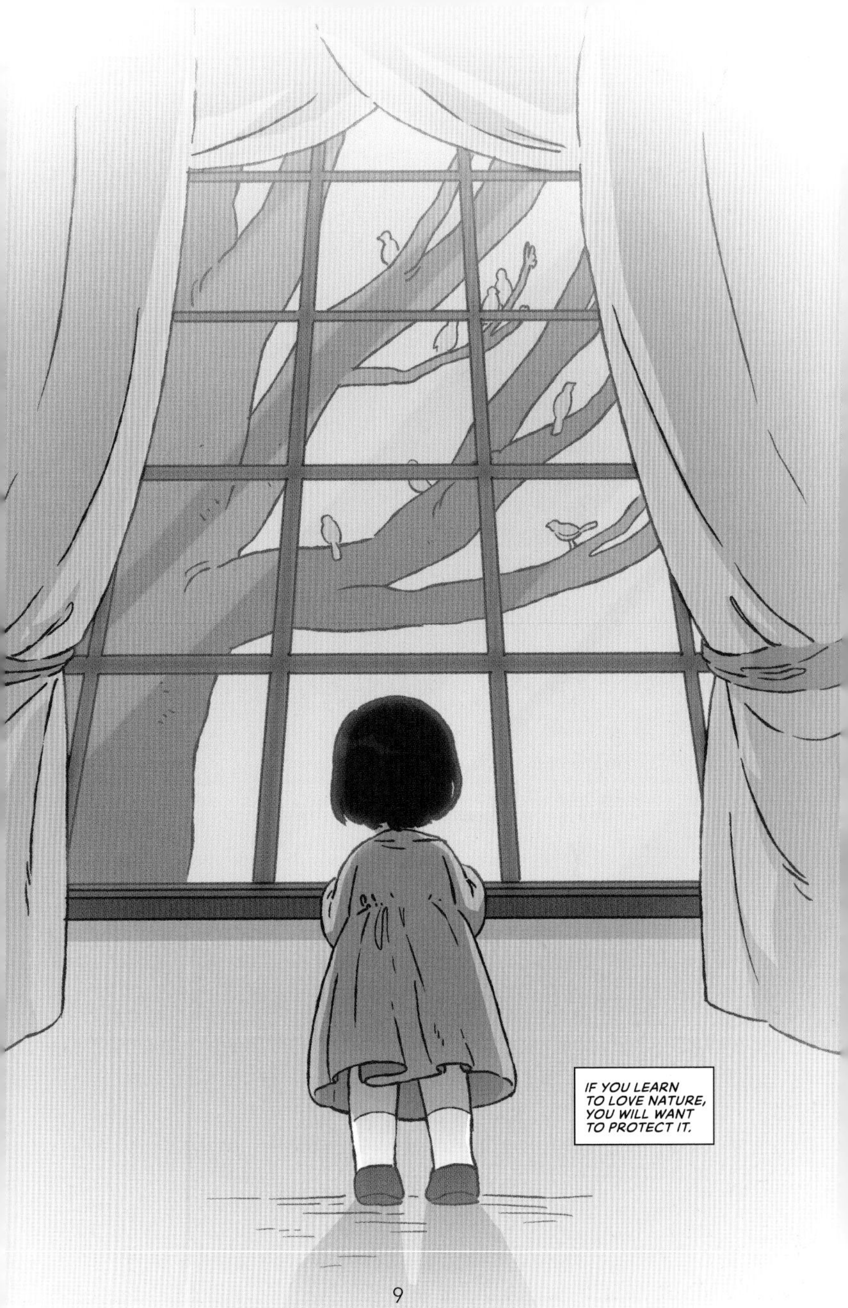
IF YOU LEARN TO LOVE NATURE, YOU WILL WANT TO PROTECT IT.

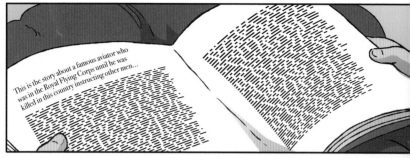

This is the story about a famous aviator who was in the Royal Flying Corps until he was killed in this country instructing other men...

"THE MAIN FACTS OF THIS STORY WERE TOLD TO ME BY MY BROTHER, WHO IS A SOLDER."

RACHEL!

LUNCHTIME!

CAN WE GO ON A WALK FIRST, MAMA?

PLEASE?

I AM A WRITER WHO ALSO LOVES NATURE.

HAHAHA! I SUPPOSE SO!

SOMEDAY, I WILL LEARN THAT BOTH INTERESTS FIT AS SNUGLY TOGETHER AS TWO GLOVED HANDS.

BUT NOT NOW.

BARK BARK

NOW IS DIFFERENT.

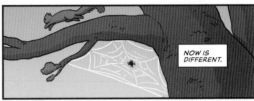

LOOK AT HOW GEOMETRIC THESE PATTERNS ARE!

AREN'T THEY MARVELOUS?

YES, INDEED!

NOW IS CALM.

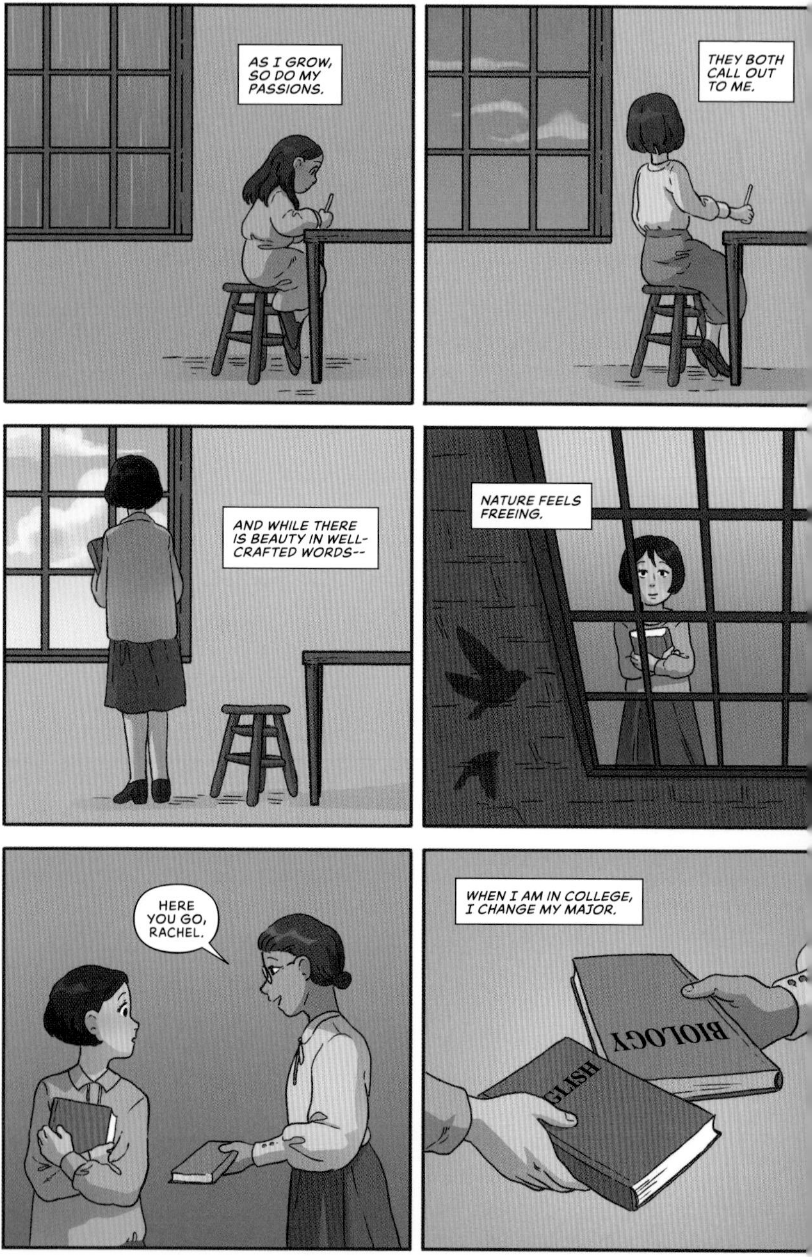
AS I GROW, SO DO MY PASSIONS.
THEY BOTH CALL OUT TO ME.
AND WHILE THERE IS BEAUTY IN WELL-CRAFTED WORDS--
NATURE FEELS FREEING.
HERE YOU GO, RACHEL.
WHEN I AM IN COLLEGE, I CHANGE MY MAJOR.
BIOLOGY
GLISH

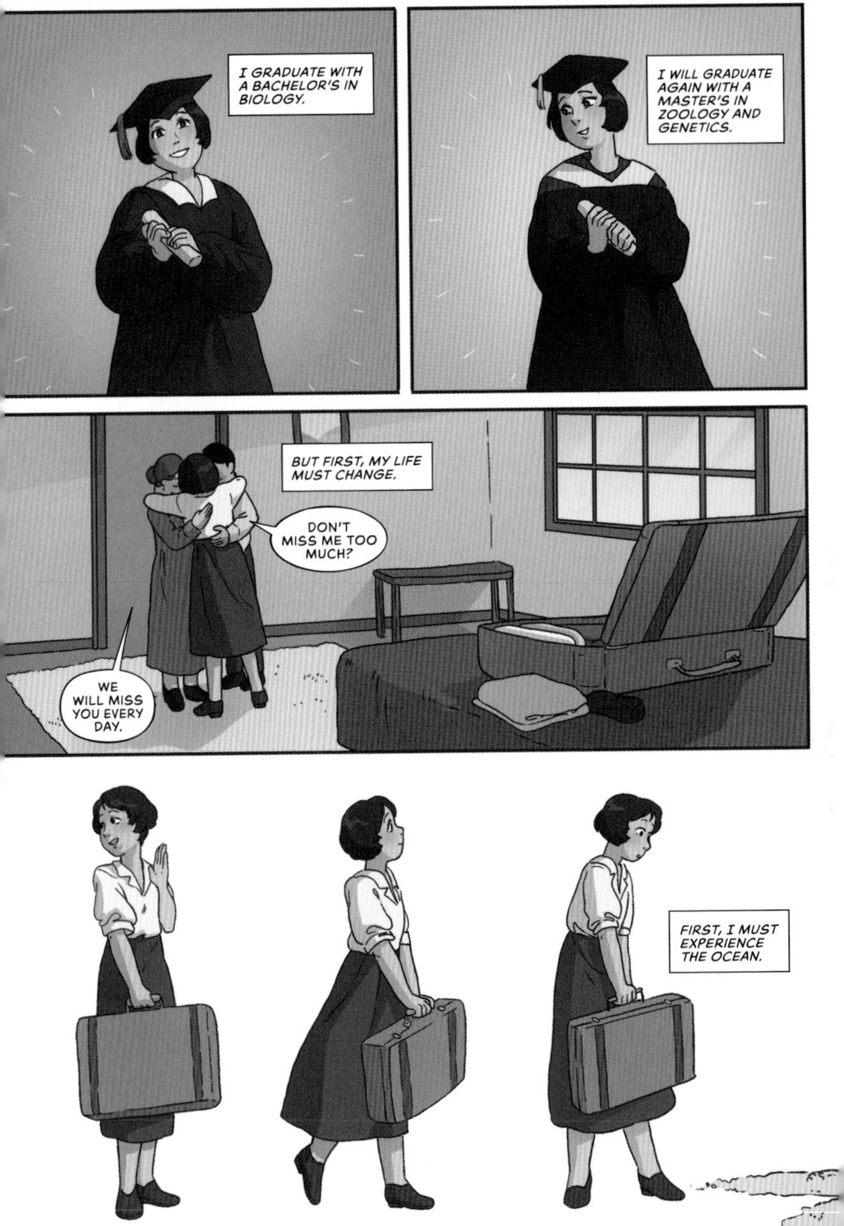
I GRADUATE WITH A BACHELOR'S IN BIOLOGY.
I WILL GRADUATE AGAIN WITH A MASTER'S IN ZOOLOGY AND GENETICS.
BUT FIRST, MY LIFE MUST CHANGE.
DON'T MISS ME TOO MUCH?
WE WILL MISS YOU EVERY DAY.
FIRST, I MUST EXPERIENCE THE OCEAN.

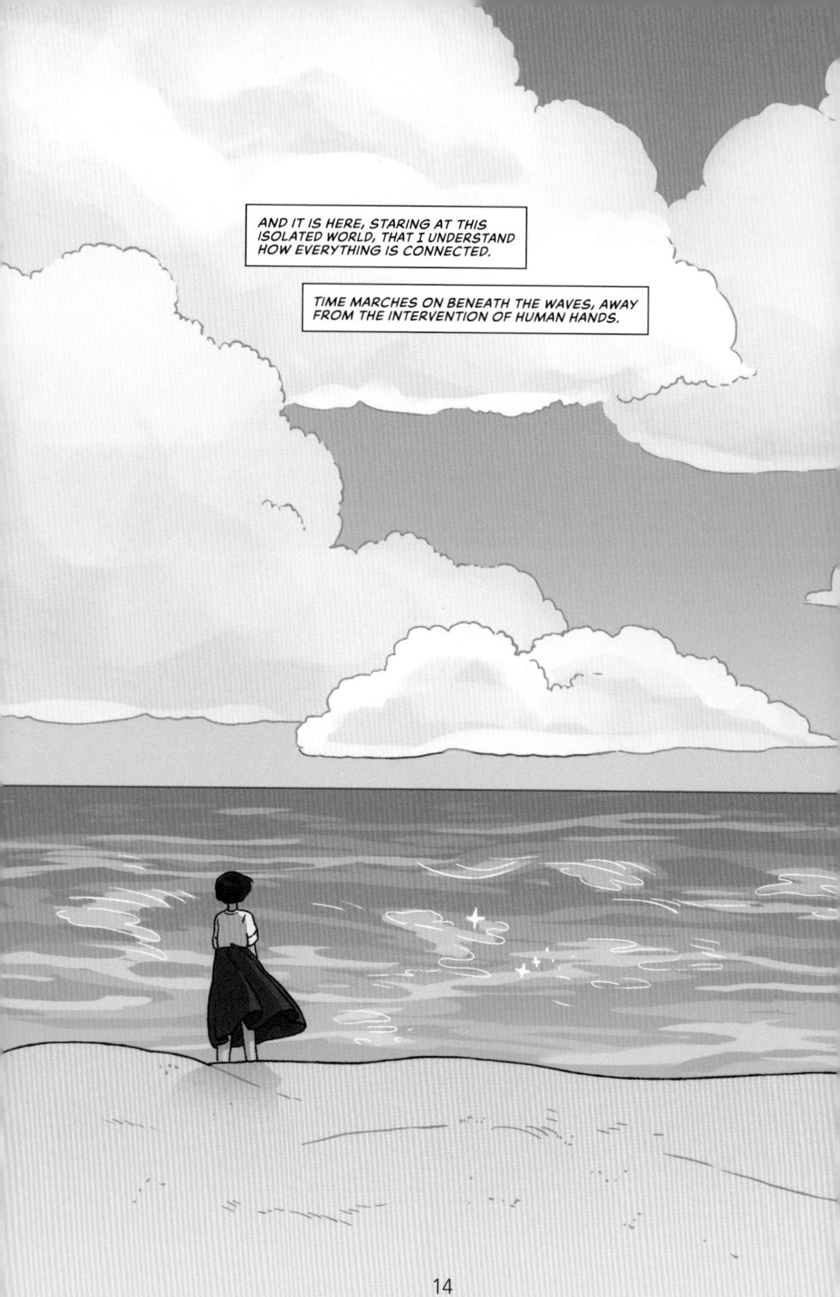
AND IT IS HERE, STARING AT THIS ISOLATED WORLD, THAT I UNDERSTAND HOW EVERYTHING IS CONNECTED.
TIME MARCHES ON BENEATH THE WAVES, AWAY FROM THE INTERVENTION OF HUMAN HANDS.

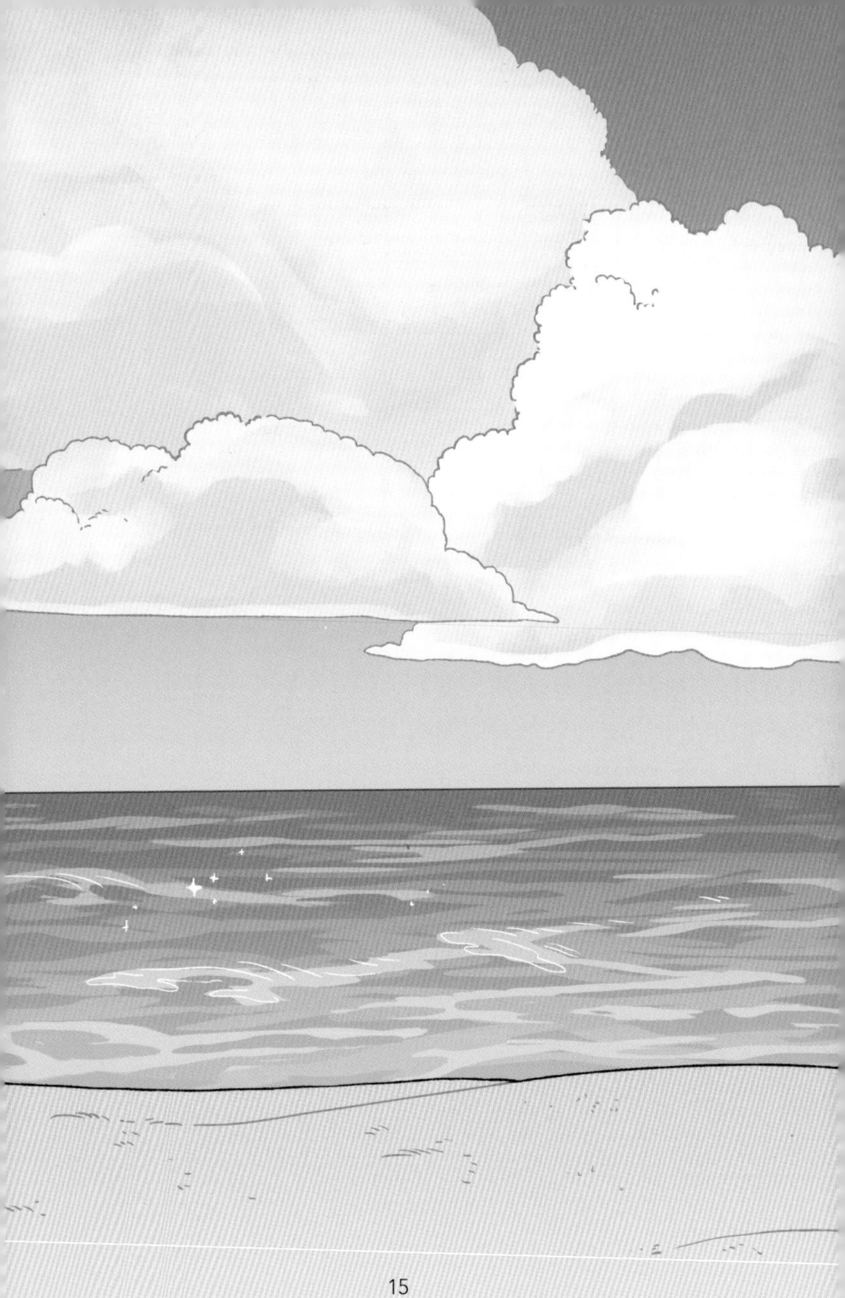

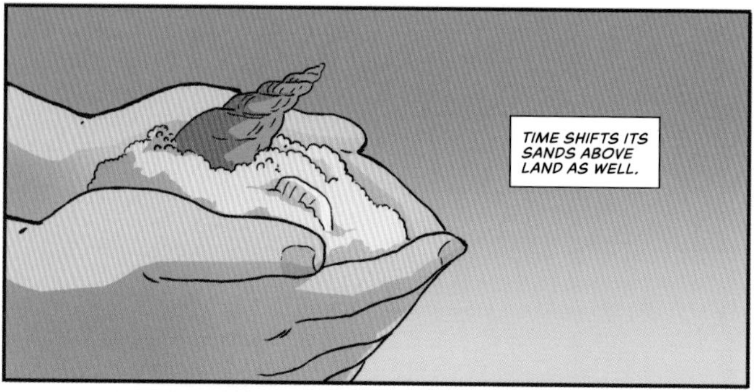
TIME SHIFTS ITS SANDS ABOVE LAND AS WELL.

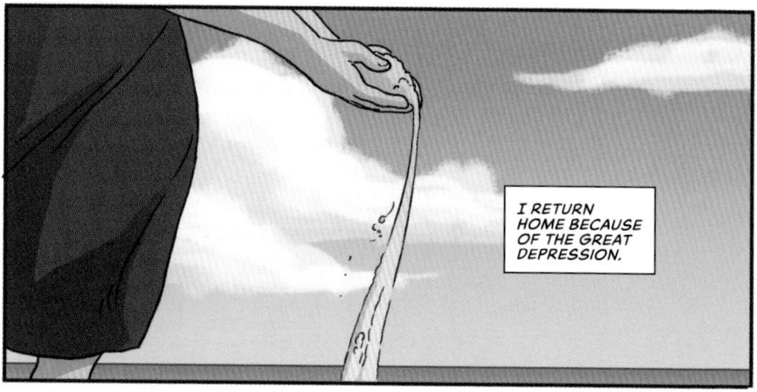
I RETURN HOME BECAUSE OF THE GREAT DEPRESSION.

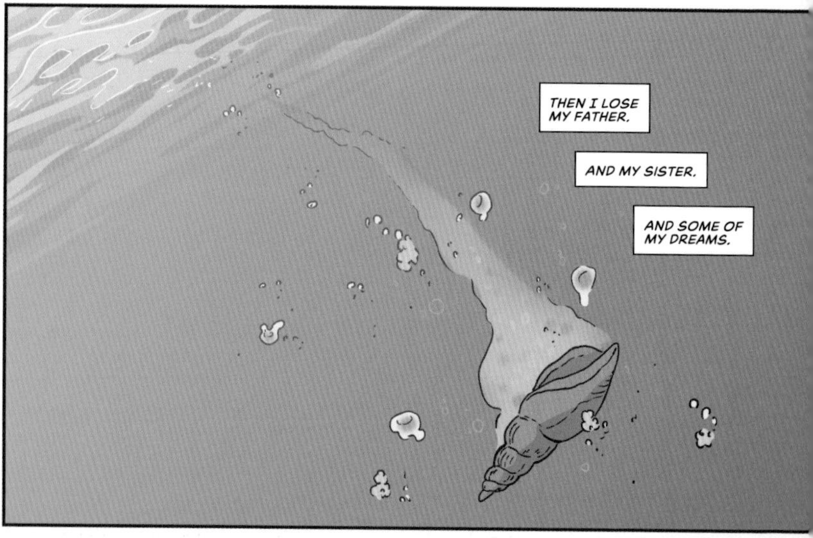
THEN I LOSE MY FATHER.
AND MY SISTER.
AND SOME OF MY DREAMS.

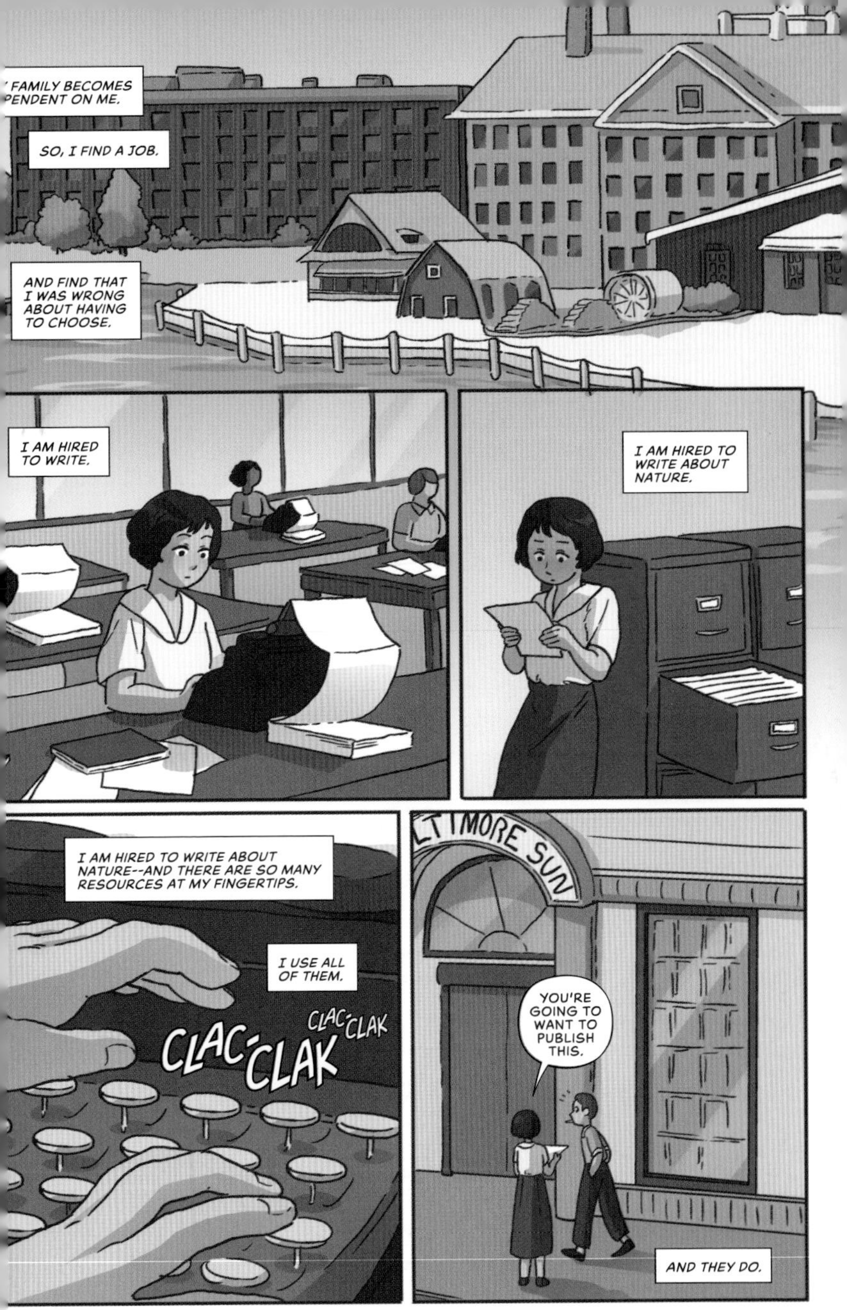
' FAMILY BECOMES
'PENDENT ON ME.
SO, I FIND A JOB.
AND FIND THAT I WAS WRONG ABOUT HAVING TO CHOOSE.
I AM HIRED TO WRITE.
I AM HIRED TO WRITE ABOUT NATURE.
I AM HIRED TO WRITE ABOUT NATURE--AND THERE ARE SO MANY RESOURCES AT MY FINGERTIPS.
I USE ALL OF THEM.
CLAC-CLAK
CLAC-CLAK
LTIMORE SUN
YOU'RE GOING TO WANT TO PUBLISH THIS.
AND THEY DO.

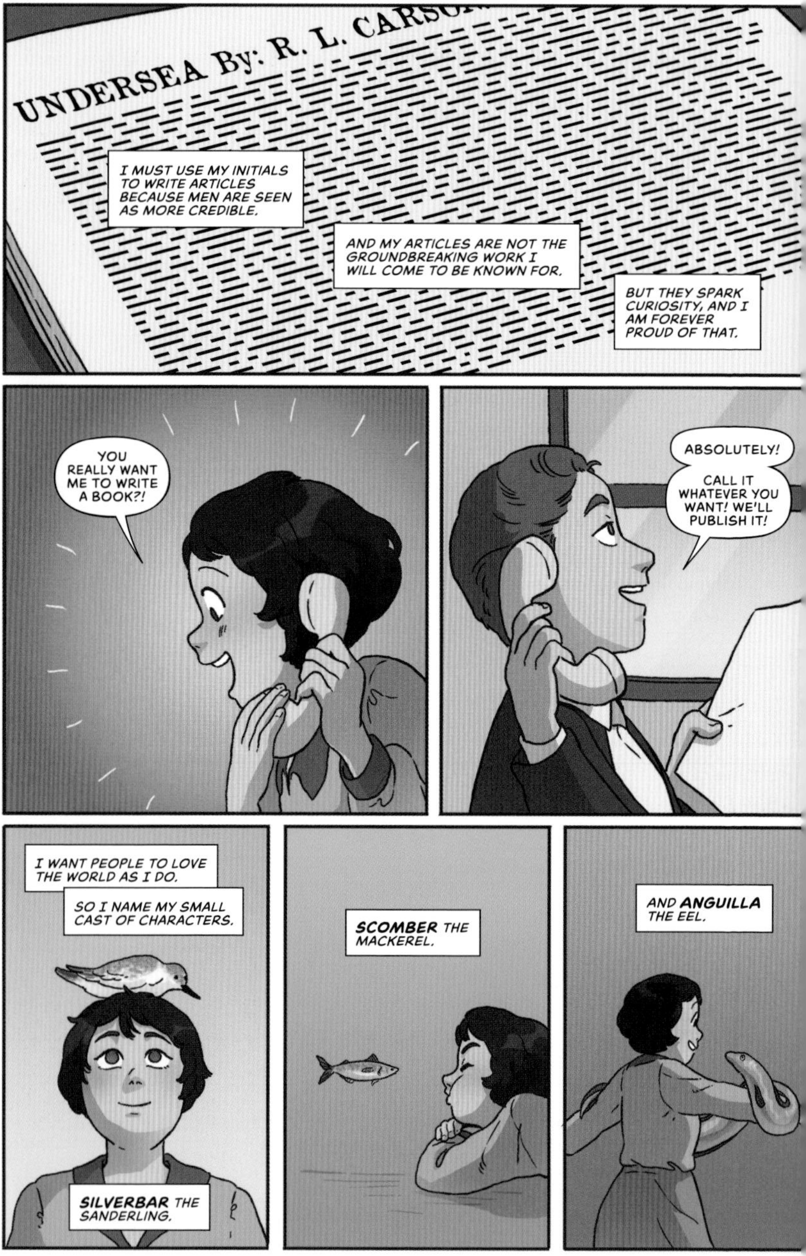
UNDERSEA By: R. L. CARSON
I MUST USE MY INITIALS TO WRITE ARTICLES BECAUSE MEN ARE SEEN AS MORE CREDIBLE.
AND MY ARTICLES ARE NOT THE GROUNDBREAKING WORK I WILL COME TO BE KNOWN FOR.
BUT THEY SPARK CURIOSITY, AND I AM FOREVER PROUD OF THAT.
YOU REALLY WANT ME TO WRITE A BOOK?!
ABSOLUTELY!
CALL IT WHATEVER YOU WANT! WE'LL PUBLISH IT!
I WANT PEOPLE TO LOVE THE WORLD AS I DO.
SO I NAME MY SMALL CAST OF CHARACTERS.
SILVERBAR THE SANDERLING.
SCOMBER THE MACKEREL.
AND ANGUILLA THE EEL.

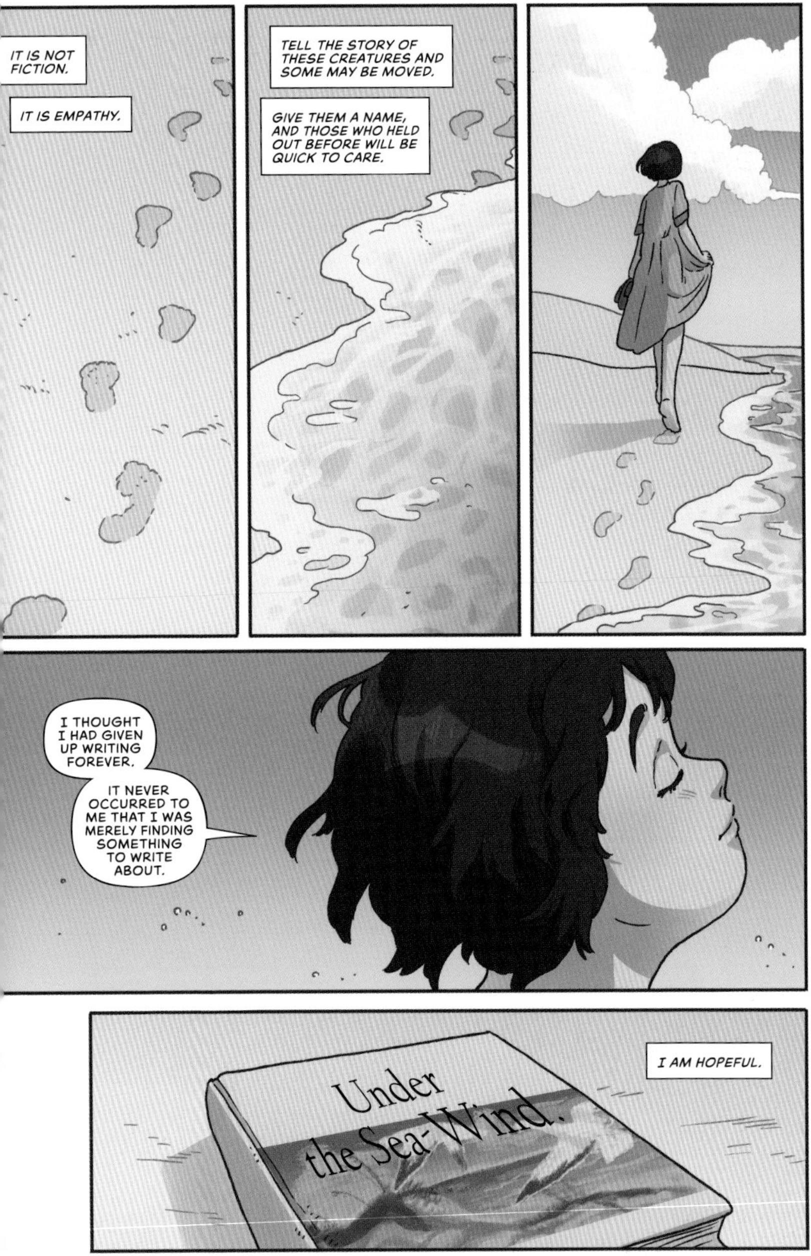
IT IS NOT FICTION.
IT IS EMPATHY.
TELL THE STORY OF THESE CREATURES AND SOME MAY BE MOVED.
GIVE THEM A NAME, AND THOSE WHO HELD OUT BEFORE WILL BE QUICK TO CARE.
I THOUGHT I HAD GIVEN UP WRITING FOREVER.
IT NEVER OCCURRED TO ME THAT I WAS MERELY FINDING SOMETHING TO WRITE ABOUT.
I AM HOPEFUL.
Under the Sea-Wind.

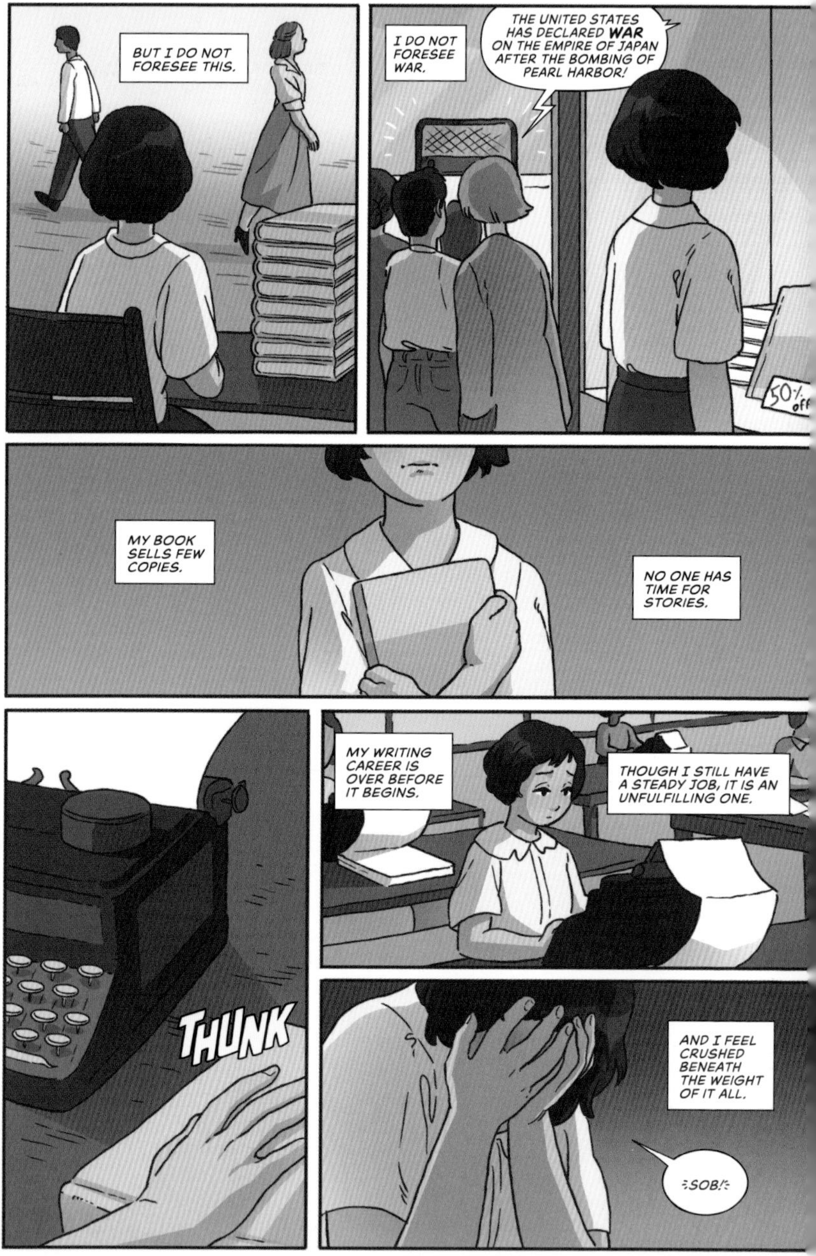
BUT I DO NOT FORESEE THIS.
I DO NOT FORESEE WAR.
THE UNITED STATES HAS DECLARED WAR ON THE EMPIRE OF JAPAN AFTER THE BOMBING OF PEARL HARBOR!
50% off
MY BOOK SELLS FEW COPIES.
NO ONE HAS TIME FOR STORIES.
THUNK
MY WRITING CAREER IS OVER BEFORE IT BEGINS.
THOUGH I STILL HAVE A STEADY JOB, IT IS AN UNFULFILLING ONE.
AND I FEEL CRUSHED BENEATH THE WEIGHT OF IT ALL.
SOB!

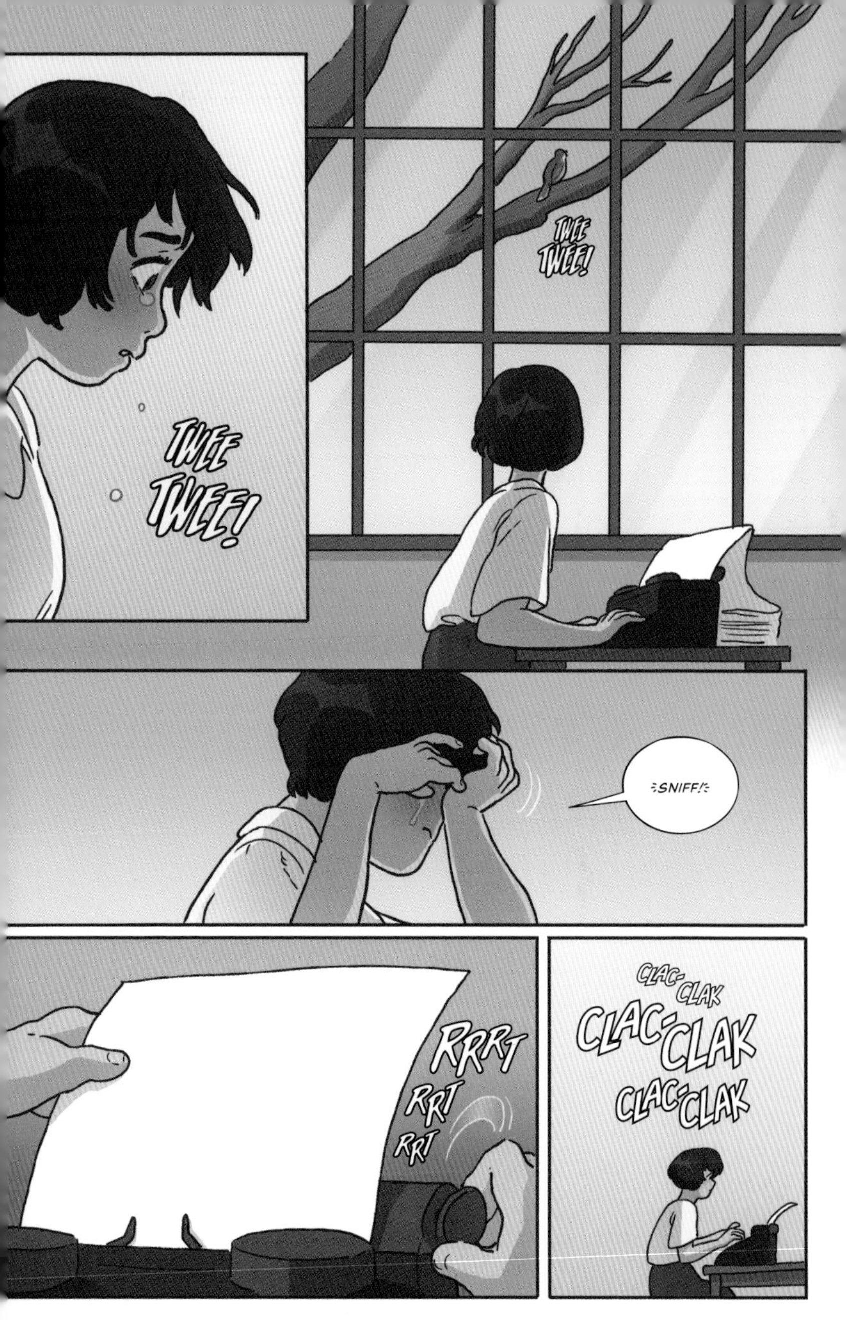
TWEE TWEE!
TWEE TWEE!
SNIFF!
RRRT RRT RRT
CLAC-CLAK
CLAC-CLAK
CLAC-CLAK

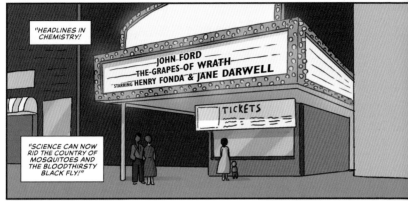

"HEADLINES IN CHEMISTRY!

JOHN FORD
THE-GRAPES-OF WRATH
STARRING HENRY FONDA & JANE DARWELL

TICKETS

"SCIENCE CAN NOW RID THE COUNTRY OF MOSQUITOES AND THE BLOODTHIRSTY BLACK FLY!"

THESE BITING INSECTS CAN BE COMPLETELY WIPED OUT BY MANMADE FOGS LOADED WITH DDT!

HAVE YOU EVER BEEN FILLED WITH THE SENSATION THAT SOMETHING IS NOT RIGHT?

PERHAPS IT SITS LOW IN YOUR BODY, SINKING YOU TO THE FLOOR.

PERHAPS IT TWITCHES UP AND DOWN YOUR SPINE IN ANXIOUS DREAD.

REGARDLESS OF THE FEELING, IF OTHERS DON'T EXPERIENCE IT TOO, YOU WILL BE IGNORED.

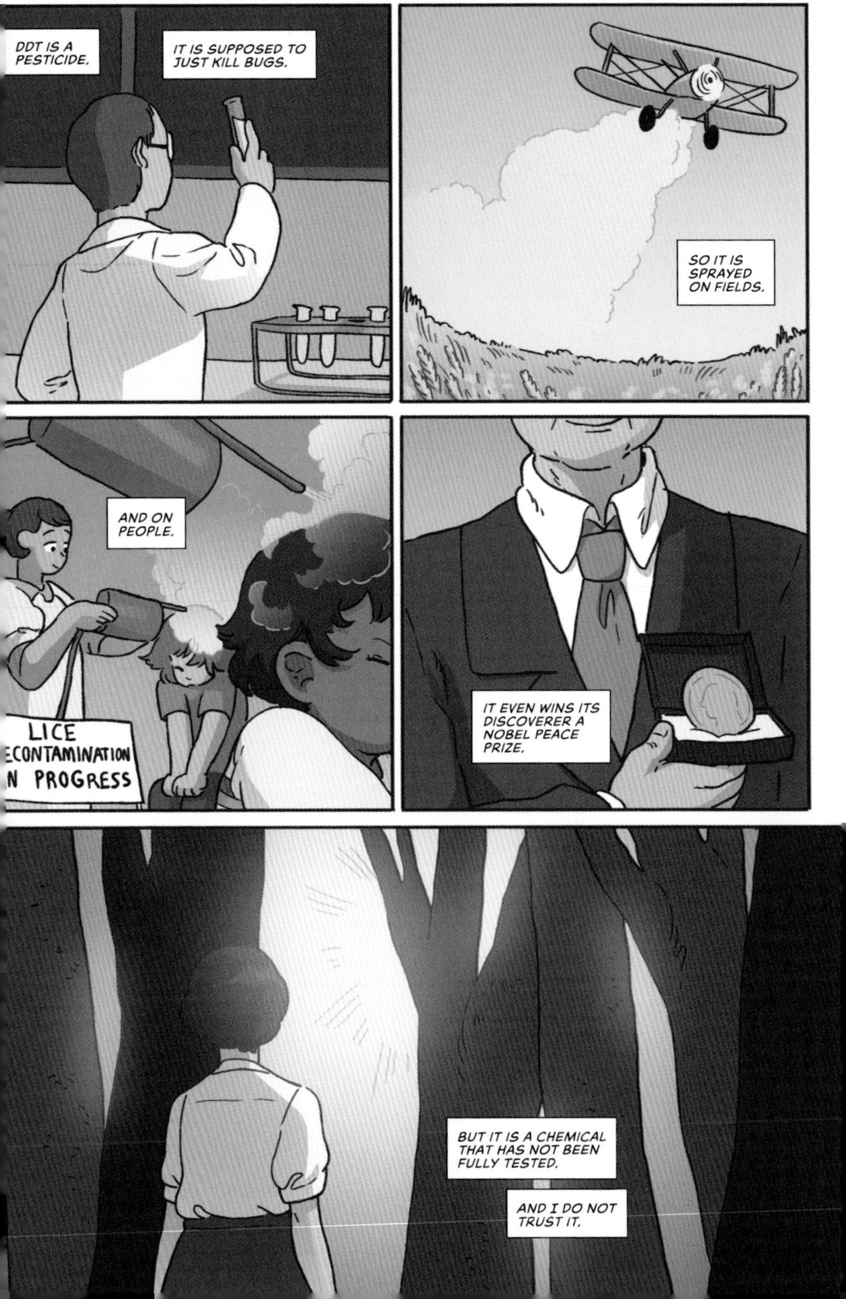
DDT IS A PESTICIDE.
IT IS SUPPOSED TO JUST KILL BUGS.
SO IT IS SPRAYED ON FIELDS.
AND ON PEOPLE.
LICE
ECONTAMINATION
N PROGRESS
IT EVEN WINS ITS DISCOVERER A NOBEL PEACE PRIZE.
BUT IT IS A CHEMICAL THAT HAS NOT BEEN FULLY TESTED.
AND I DO NOT TRUST IT.

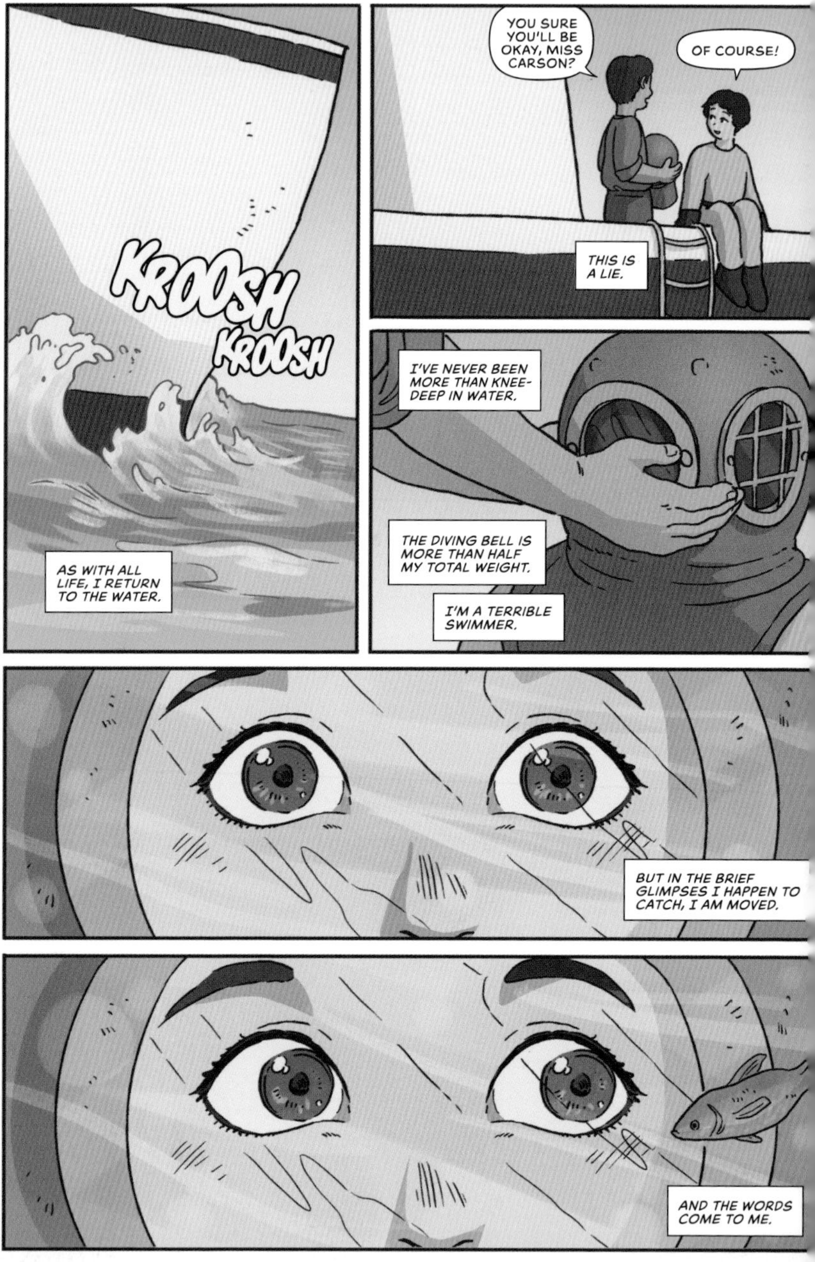
KROOSH
KROOSH
AS WITH ALL LIFE, I RETURN TO THE WATER.
YOU SURE YOU'LL BE OKAY, MISS CARSON?
OF COURSE!
THIS IS A LIE.
I'VE NEVER BEEN MORE THAN KNEE-DEEP IN WATER.
THE DIVING BELL IS MORE THAN HALF MY TOTAL WEIGHT.
I'M A TERRIBLE SWIMMER.
BUT IN THE BRIEF GLIMPSES I HAPPEN TO CATCH, I AM MOVED.
AND THE WORDS COME TO ME.

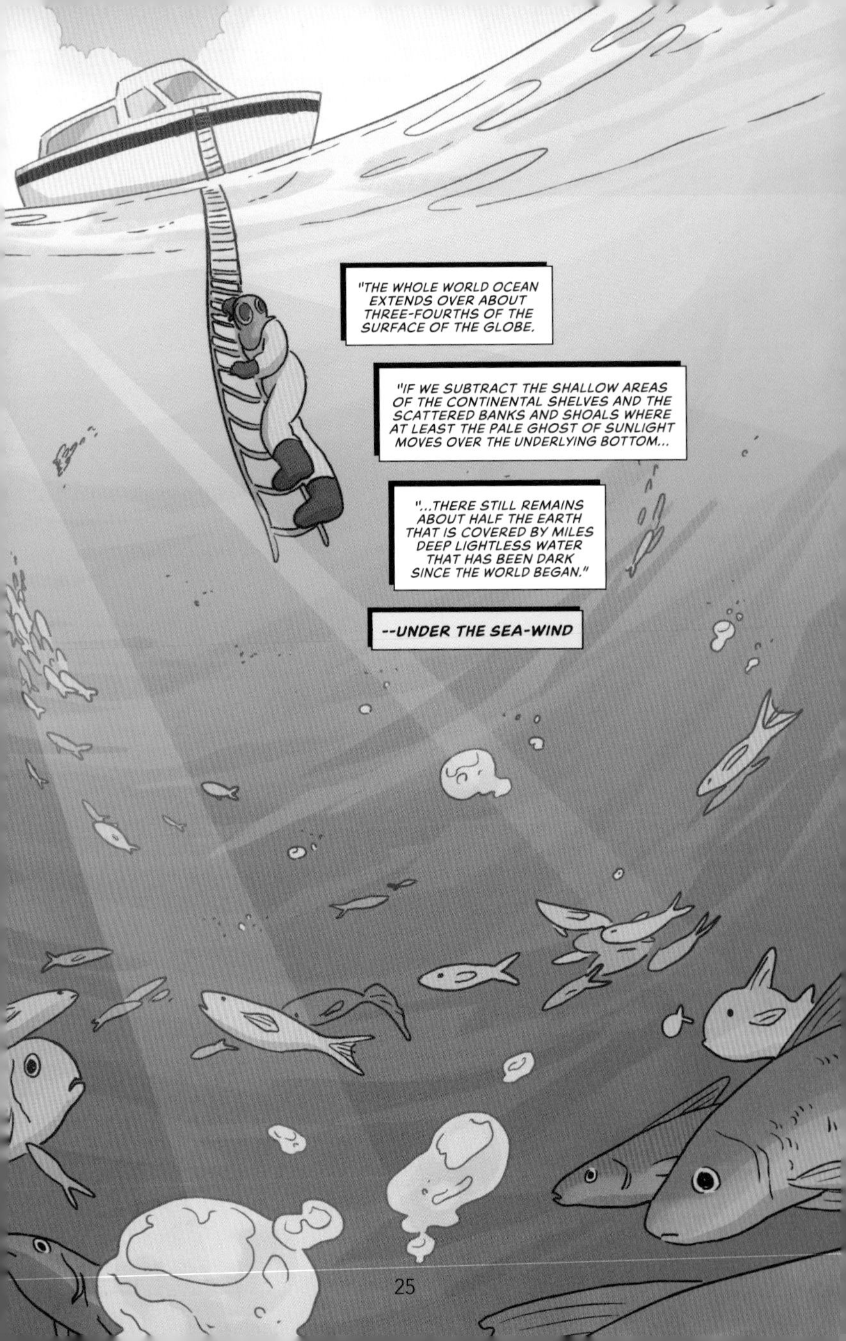
"THE WHOLE WORLD OCEAN EXTENDS OVER ABOUT THREE-FOURTHS OF THE SURFACE OF THE GLOBE.
"IF WE SUBTRACT THE SHALLOW AREAS OF THE CONTINENTAL SHELVES AND THE SCATTERED BANKS AND SHOALS WHERE AT LEAST THE PALE GHOST OF SUNLIGHT MOVES OVER THE UNDERLYING BOTTOM...
"...THERE STILL REMAINS ABOUT HALF THE EARTH THAT IS COVERED BY MILES DEEP LIGHTLESS WATER THAT HAS BEEN DARK SINCE THE WORLD BEGAN."
--UNDER THE SEA-WIND

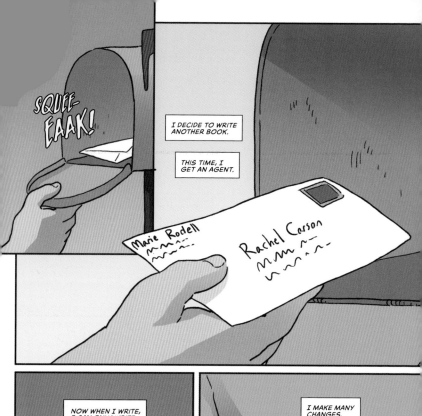

SQUEE-EAAK!

I DECIDE TO WRITE ANOTHER BOOK.

THIS TIME, I GET AN AGENT.

Marie Rodell

Rachel Carson

NOW WHEN I WRITE, I CAN ONLY WRITE ONE SENTENCE AT A TIME. EACH ONE MUST BE PERFECT.

I MAKE MANY CHANGES.

THEY ARE NOT ALL TO THE BOOK.

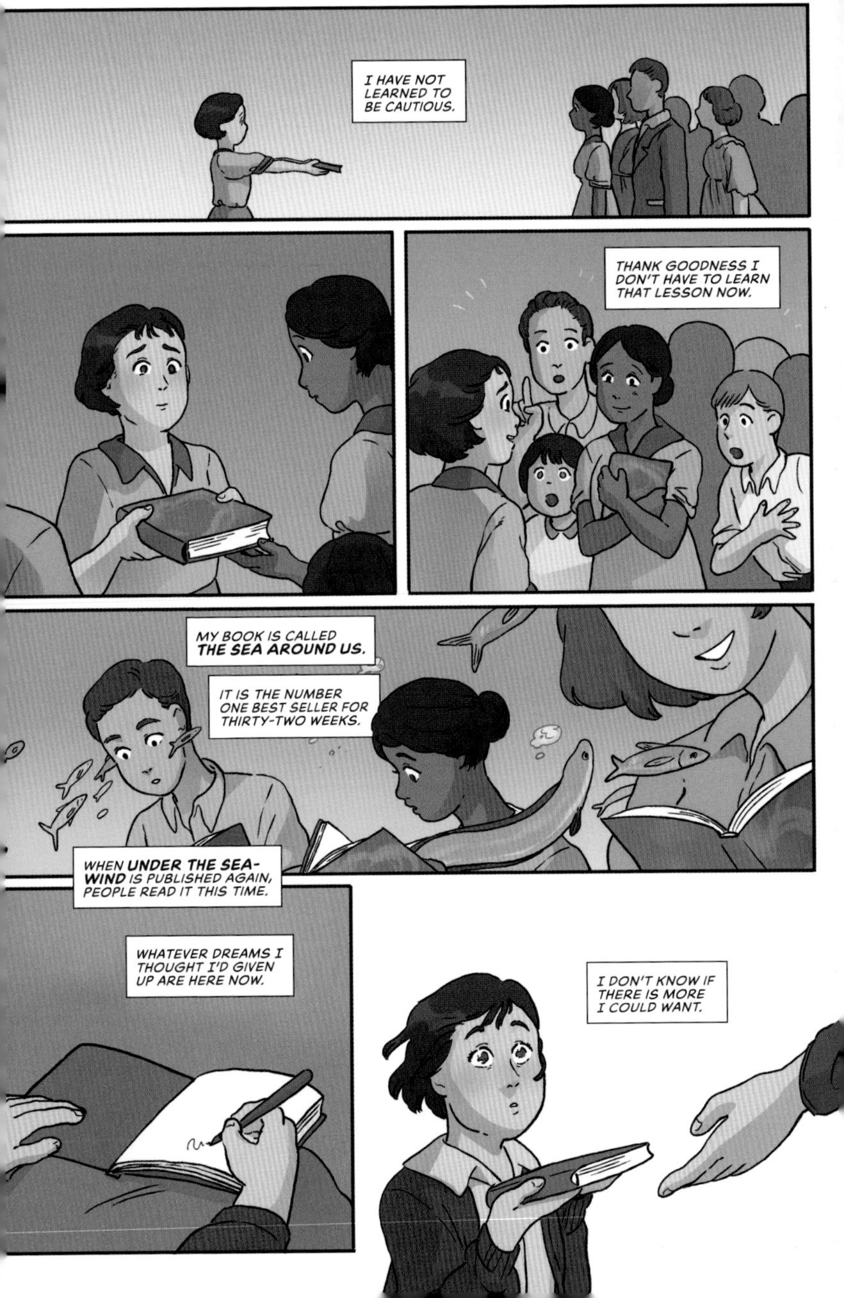
I HAVE NOT LEARNED TO BE CAUTIOUS.
THANK GOODNESS I DON'T HAVE TO LEARN THAT LESSON NOW.
MY BOOK IS CALLED **THE SEA AROUND US**.
IT IS THE NUMBER ONE BEST SELLER FOR THIRTY-TWO WEEKS.
WHEN **UNDER THE SEA-WIND** IS PUBLISHED AGAIN, PEOPLE READ IT THIS TIME.
WHATEVER DREAMS I THOUGHT I'D GIVEN UP ARE HERE NOW.
I DON'T KNOW IF THERE IS MORE I COULD WANT.

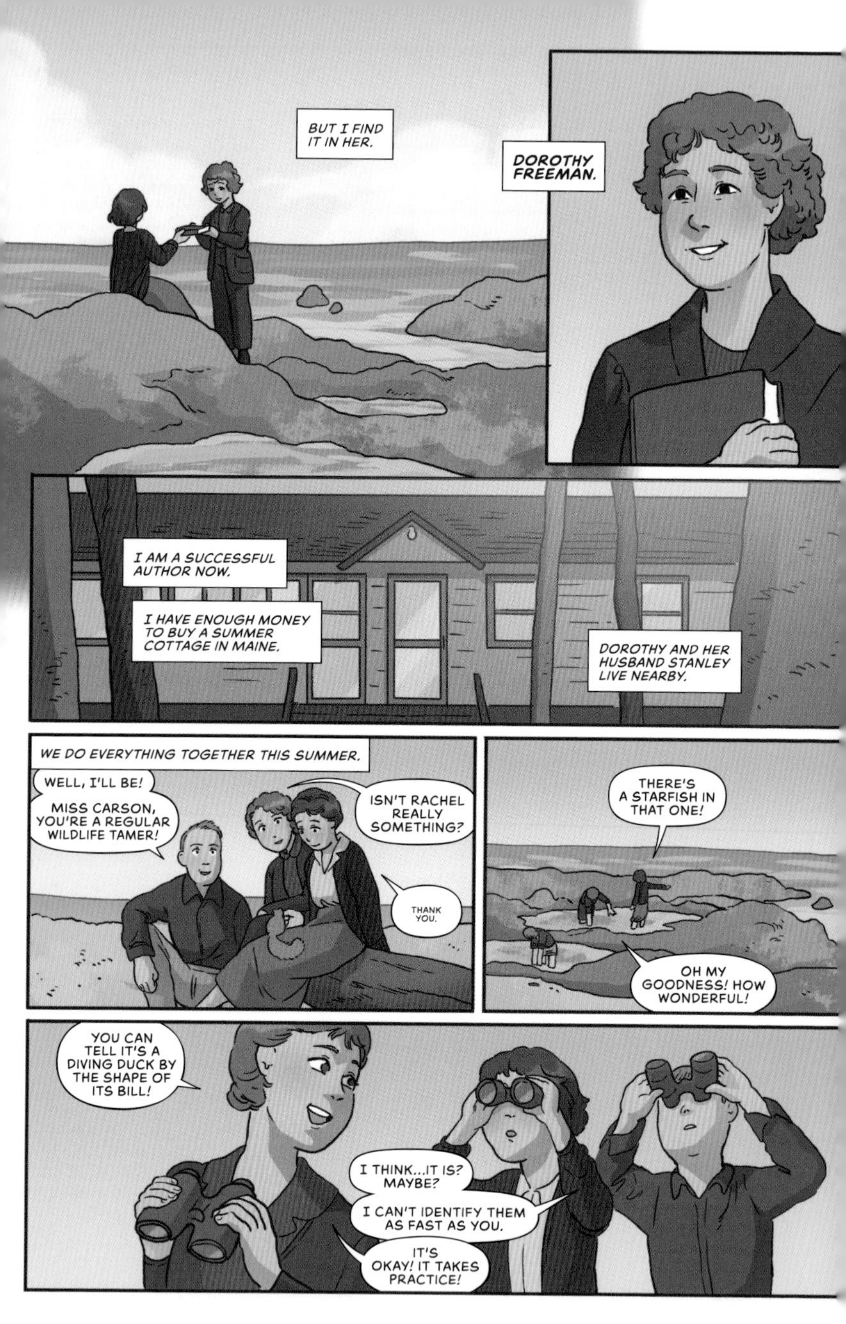
BUT I FIND IT IN HER.
DOROTHY FREEMAN.
I AM A SUCCESSFUL AUTHOR NOW.
I HAVE ENOUGH MONEY TO BUY A SUMMER COTTAGE IN MAINE.
DOROTHY AND HER HUSBAND STANLEY LIVE NEARBY.
WE DO EVERYTHING TOGETHER THIS SUMMER.
WELL, I'LL BE!
MISS CARSON, YOU'RE A REGULAR WILDLIFE TAMER!
ISN'T RACHEL REALLY SOMETHING?
THANK YOU.
THERE'S A STARFISH IN THAT ONE!
OH MY GOODNESS! HOW WONDERFUL!
YOU CAN TELL IT'S A DIVING DUCK BY THE SHAPE OF ITS BILL!
I THINK...IT IS? MAYBE?
I CAN'T IDENTIFY THEM AS FAST AS YOU.
IT'S OKAY! IT TAKES PRACTICE!

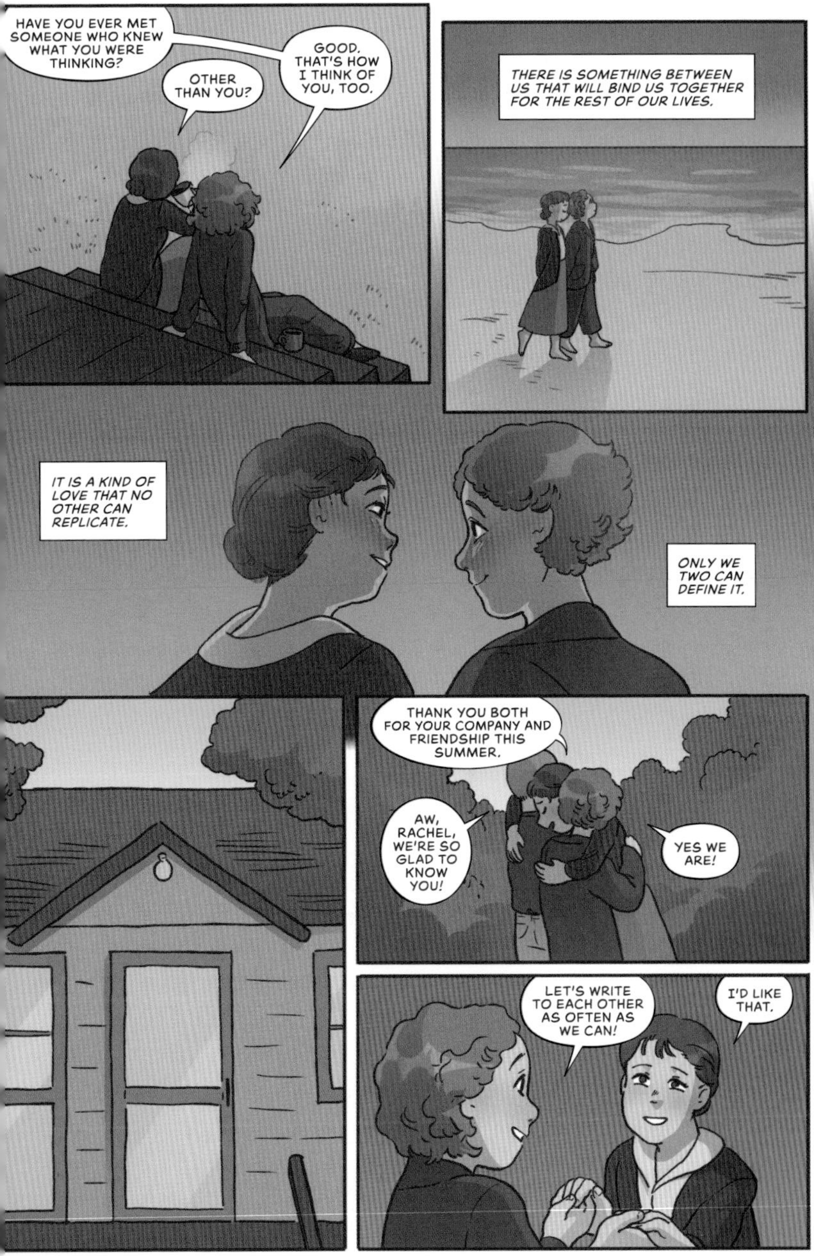
HAVE YOU EVER MET SOMEONE WHO KNEW WHAT YOU WERE THINKING?
OTHER THAN YOU?
GOOD. THAT'S HOW I THINK OF YOU, TOO.
THERE IS SOMETHING BETWEEN US THAT WILL BIND US TOGETHER FOR THE REST OF OUR LIVES.
IT IS A KIND OF LOVE THAT NO OTHER CAN REPLICATE.
ONLY WE TWO CAN DEFINE IT.
THANK YOU BOTH FOR YOUR COMPANY AND FRIENDSHIP THIS SUMMER.
AW, RACHEL, WE'RE SO GLAD TO KNOW YOU!
YES WE ARE!
LET'S WRITE TO EACH OTHER AS OFTEN AS WE CAN!
I'D LIKE THAT.

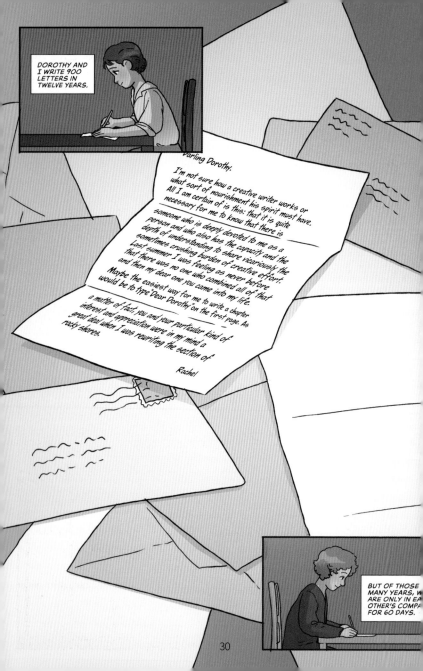

DOROTHY AND I WRITE 900 LETTERS IN TWELVE YEARS.

Darling Dorothy:

I'm not sure how a creative writer works or what sort of nourishment his spirit must have. All I am certain of is this: that it is quite necessary for me to know that there is _____ someone who is deeply devoted to me as a person and who also has the capacity and the depth of understanding to share vicariously the sometimes crushing burden of creative effort: Last summer I was feeling as never before that there was no one who combined all of that and then my dear one you came into my life.

Maybe the easiest way for me to write a chapter would be to type "Dear Dorothy" on the first page. As a matter of fact, you and your particular kind of interest and appreciation were in my mind a great deal when I was rewriting the section of rocky shores.

Rachel

BUT OF THOSE MANY YEARS, W ARE ONLY IN EA OTHER'S COMPA FOR 60 DAYS.

30

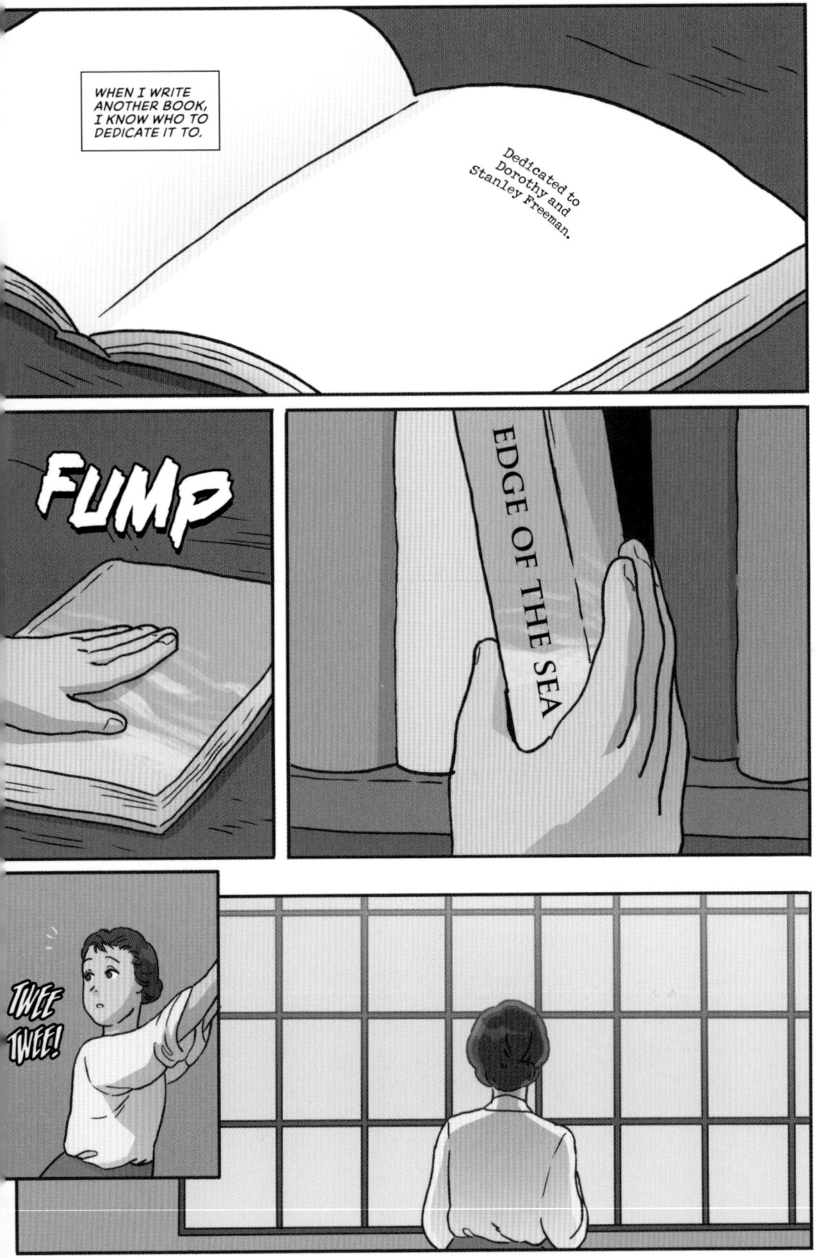
WHEN I WRITE ANOTHER BOOK, I KNOW WHO TO DEDICATE IT TO.
Dedicated to Dorothy and Stanley Freeman.
FUMP
EDGE OF THE SEA
TWEE TWEE!

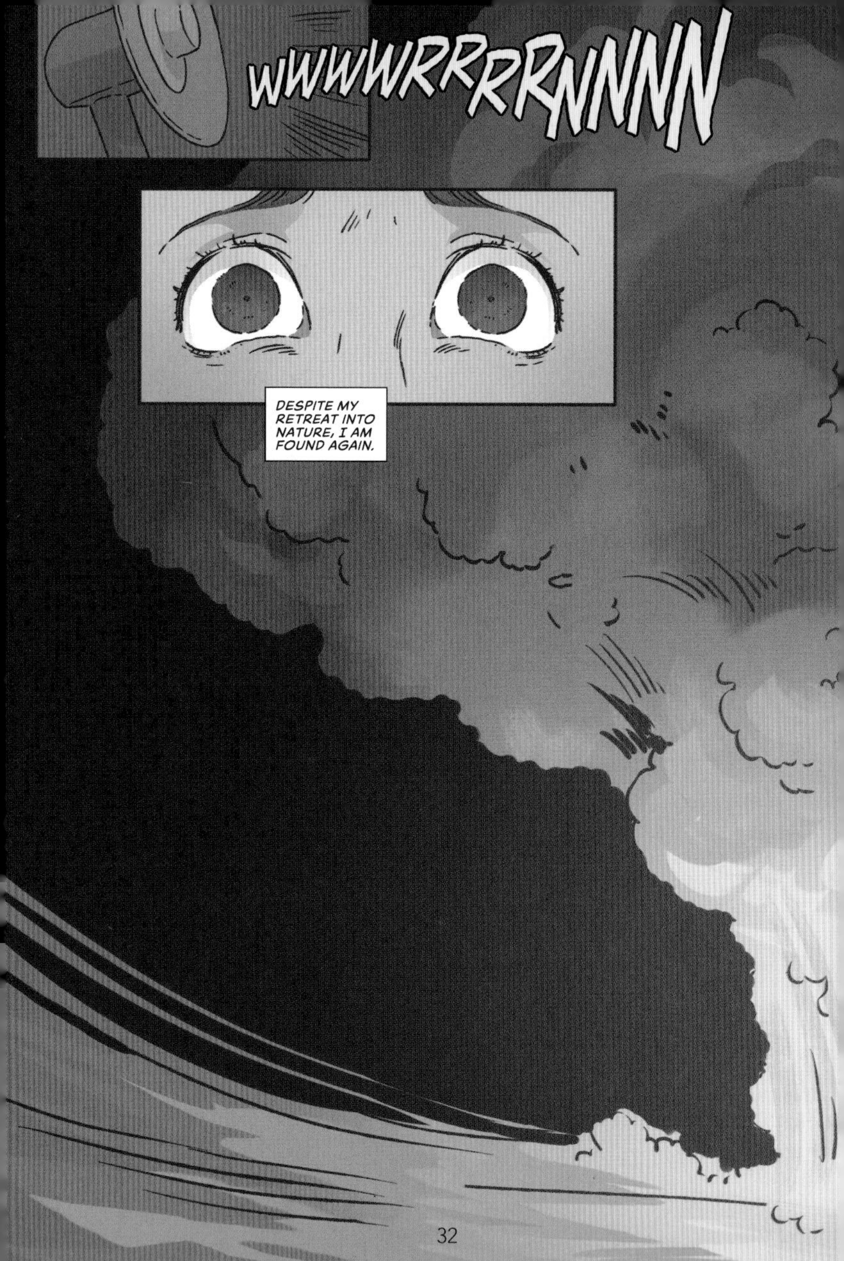
WWWWRRRRRNNNNN
DESPITE MY RETREAT INTO NATURE, I AM FOUND AGAIN.

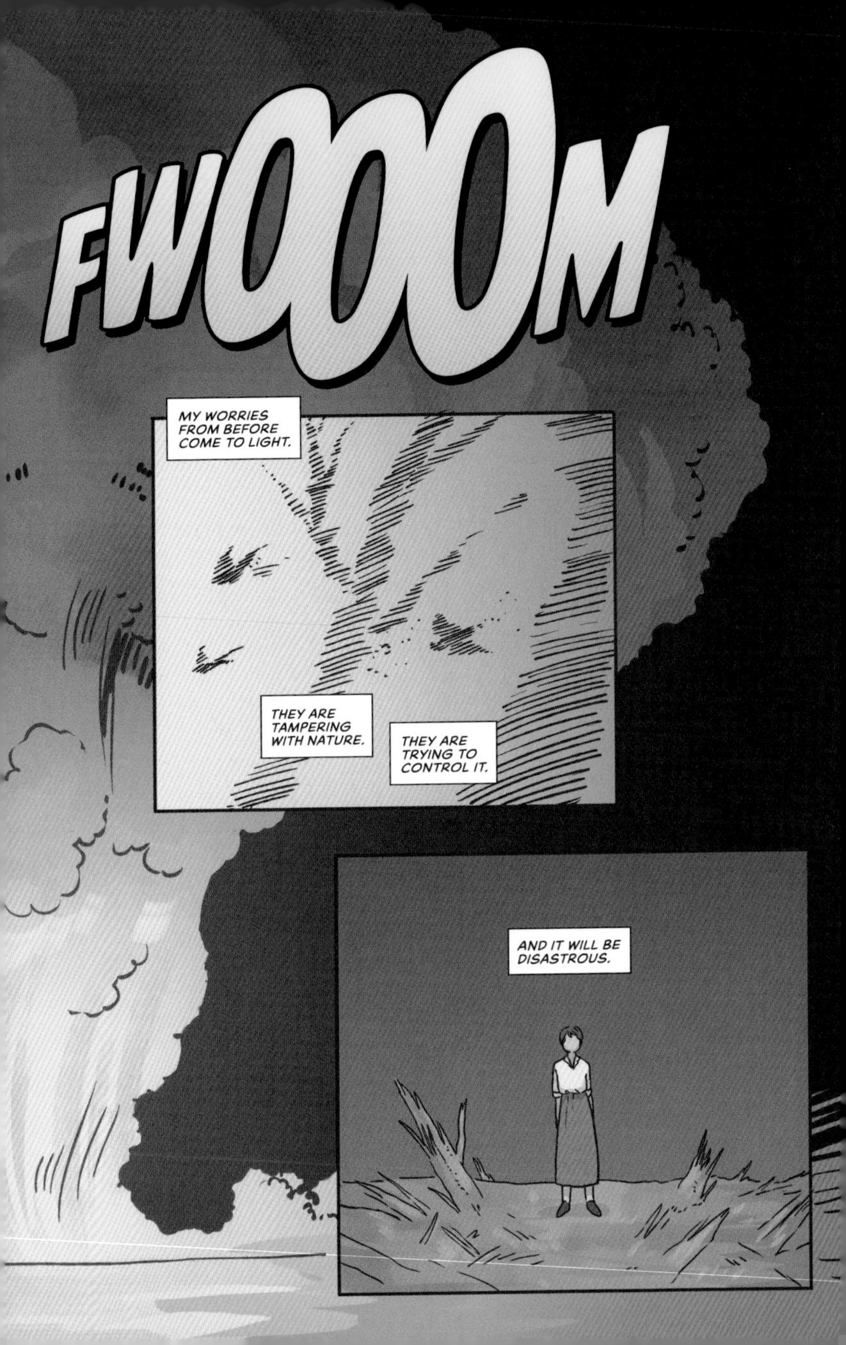
FWOOOM
MY WORRIES FROM BEFORE COME TO LIGHT.
THEY ARE TAMPERING WITH NATURE.
THEY ARE TRYING TO CONTROL IT.
AND IT WILL BE DISASTROUS.

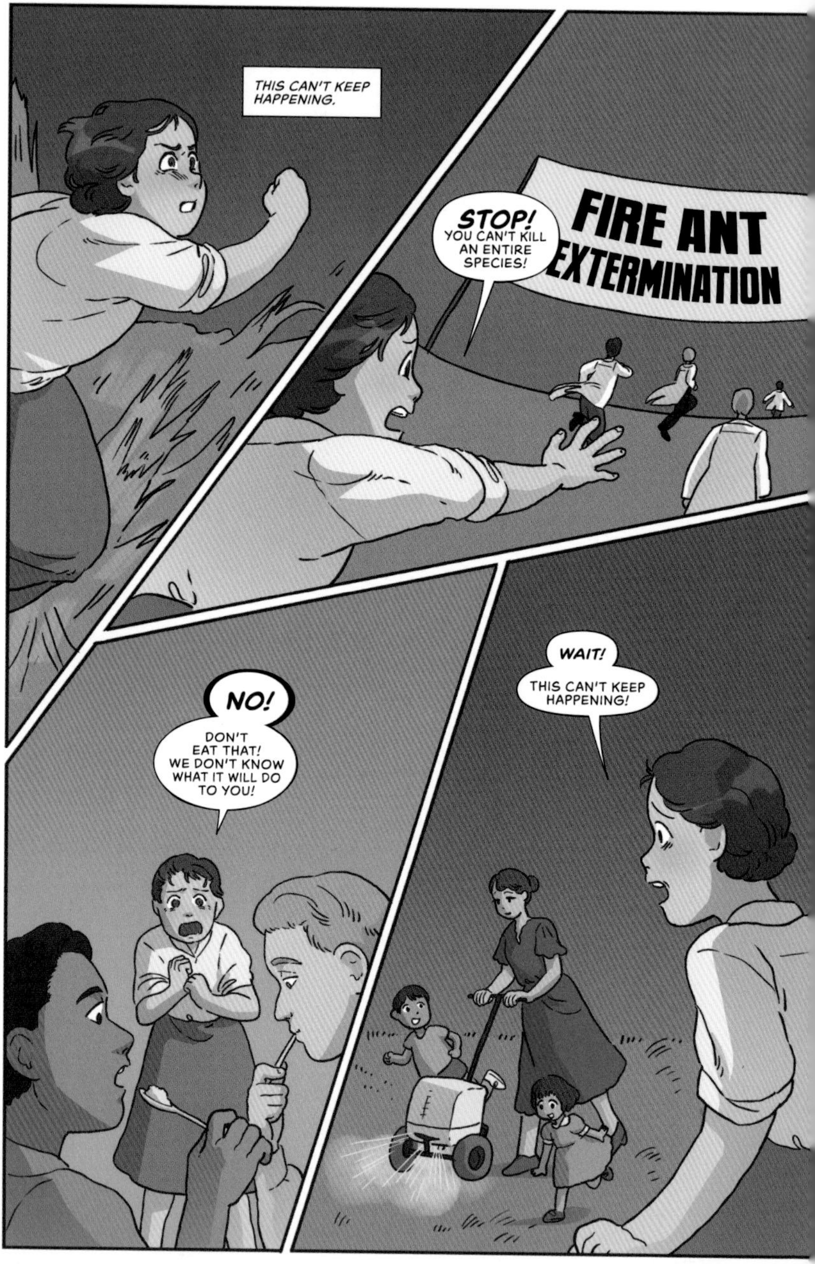

THIS CAN'T KEEP HAPPENING.
STOP! YOU CAN'T KILL AN ENTIRE SPECIES!
FIRE ANT EXTERMINATION
NO!
DON'T EAT THAT! WE DON'T KNOW WHAT IT WILL DO TO YOU!
WAIT!
THIS CAN'T KEEP HAPPENING!

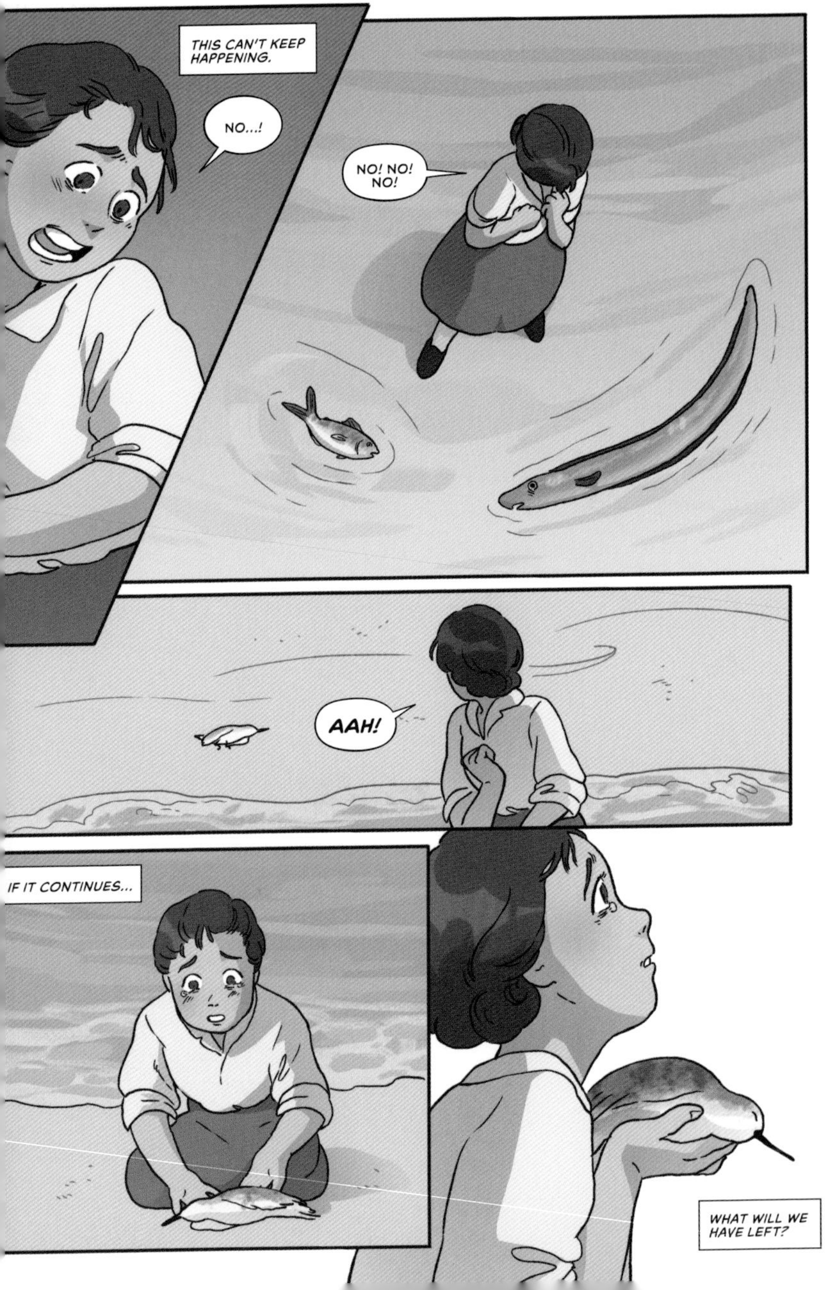
THIS CAN'T KEEP HAPPENING.
NO...!
NO! NO! NO!
AAH!
IF IT CONTINUES...
WHAT WILL WE HAVE LEFT?

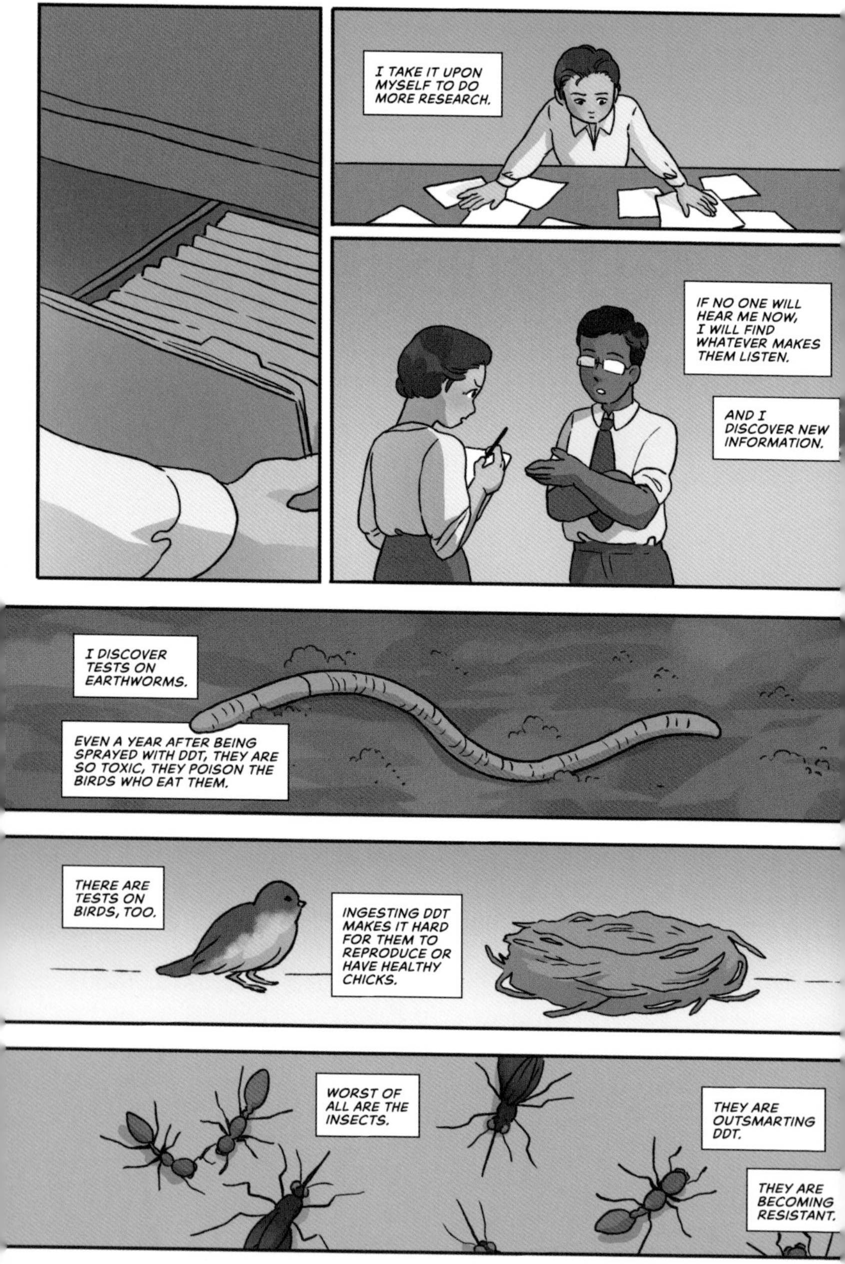
I TAKE IT UPON MYSELF TO DO MORE RESEARCH.
IF NO ONE WILL HEAR ME NOW, I WILL FIND WHATEVER MAKES THEM LISTEN.
AND I DISCOVER NEW INFORMATION.
I DISCOVER TESTS ON EARTHWORMS.
EVEN A YEAR AFTER BEING SPRAYED WITH DDT, THEY ARE SO TOXIC, THEY POISON THE BIRDS WHO EAT THEM.
THERE ARE TESTS ON BIRDS, TOO.
INGESTING DDT MAKES IT HARD FOR THEM TO REPRODUCE OR HAVE HEALTHY CHICKS.
WORST OF ALL ARE THE INSECTS.
THEY ARE OUTSMARTING DDT.
THEY ARE BECOMING RESISTANT.

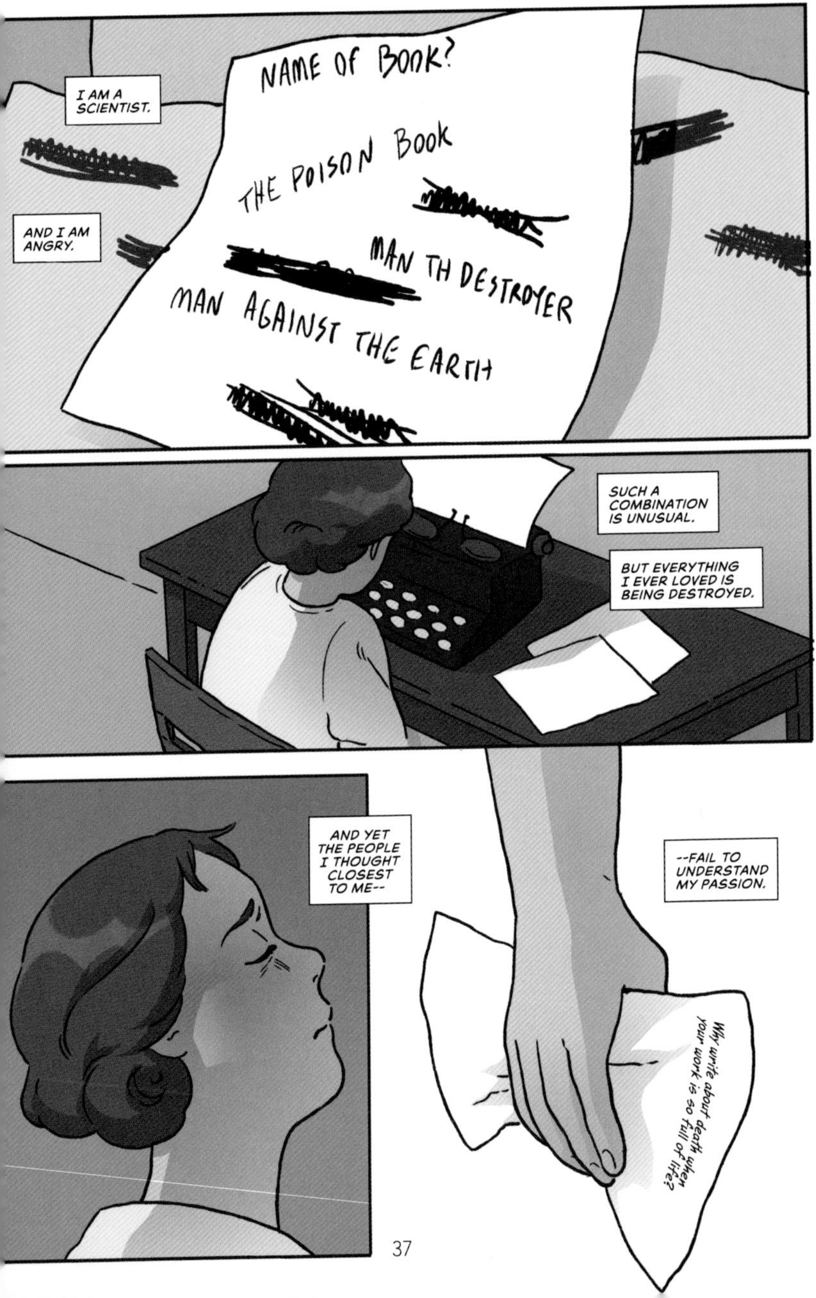
NAME OF BOOK?
THE POISON BOOK
MAN TH DESTROYER
MAN AGAINST THE EARTH
I AM A SCIENTIST.
AND I AM ANGRY.
SUCH A COMBINATION IS UNUSUAL.
BUT EVERYTHING I EVER LOVED IS BEING DESTROYED.
AND YET THE PEOPLE I THOUGHT CLOSEST TO ME--
--FAIL TO UNDERSTAND MY PASSION.
Why write about death when your work is so full of life?

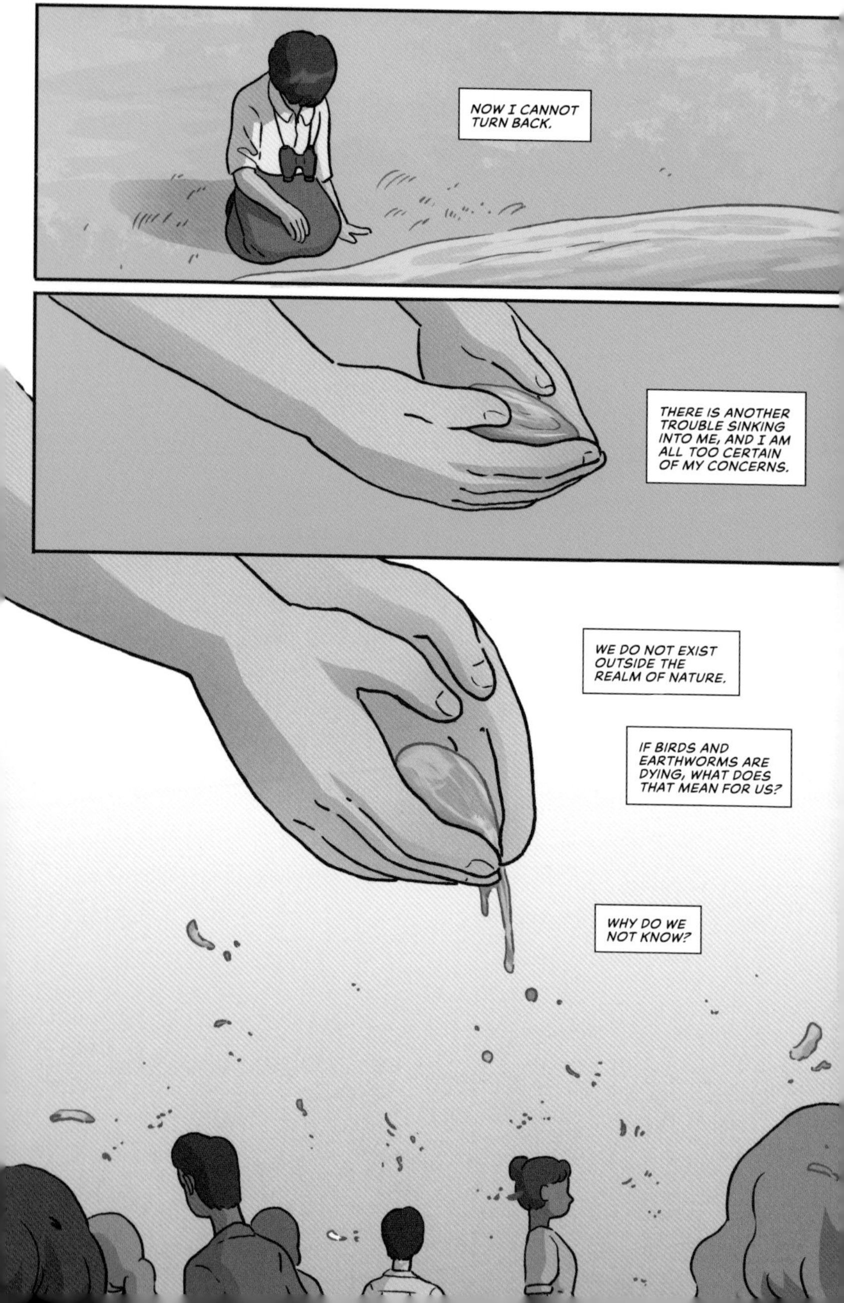
NOW I CANNOT TURN BACK.
THERE IS ANOTHER TROUBLE SINKING INTO ME, AND I AM ALL TOO CERTAIN OF MY CONCERNS.
WE DO NOT EXIST OUTSIDE THE REALM OF NATURE.
IF BIRDS AND EARTHWORMS ARE DYING, WHAT DOES THAT MEAN FOR US?
WHY DO WE NOT KNOW?

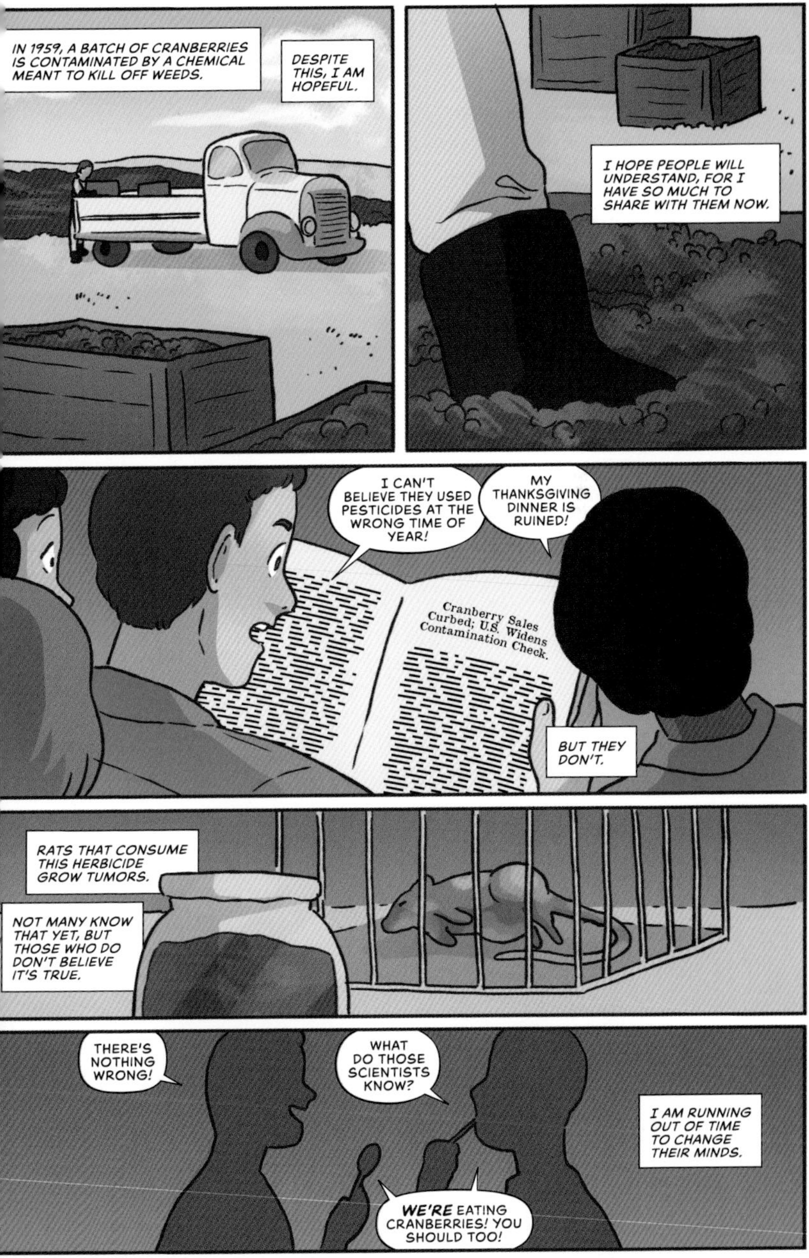
IN 1959, A BATCH OF CRANBERRIES IS CONTAMINATED BY A CHEMICAL MEANT TO KILL OFF WEEDS.
DESPITE THIS, I AM HOPEFUL.
I HOPE PEOPLE WILL UNDERSTAND, FOR I HAVE SO MUCH TO SHARE WITH THEM NOW.
I CAN'T BELIEVE THEY USED PESTICIDES AT THE WRONG TIME OF YEAR!
MY THANKSGIVING DINNER IS RUINED!
Cranberry Sales Curbed; U.S. Widens Contamination Check.
BUT THEY DON'T.
RATS THAT CONSUME THIS HERBICIDE GROW TUMORS.
NOT MANY KNOW THAT YET, BUT THOSE WHO DO DON'T BELIEVE IT'S TRUE.
THERE'S NOTHING WRONG!
WHAT DO THOSE SCIENTISTS KNOW?
I AM RUNNING OUT OF TIME TO CHANGE THEIR MINDS.
WE'RE EATING CRANBERRIES! YOU SHOULD TOO!

INSIDE, I CARRY A DEADLY SECRET.

IF ANYONE FIGURES IT OUT, MY BOOK WILL BE COMPROMISED.

I CAN'T LET THEM. IT WILL ONLY BE SEEN AS A BITTER TOME ABOUT DEATH.

NO ONE WILL UNDERSTAND IT IS A PASSION FOR LIFE THAT DRIVES MY WORK.

BUT FOR MONTHS, I AM CONFINED TO BED,

I CAN BARELY WALK.

I CAN'T WRITE AT ALL.

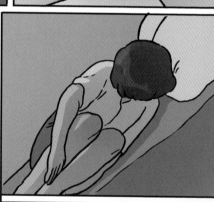

AND I AM TIRED.

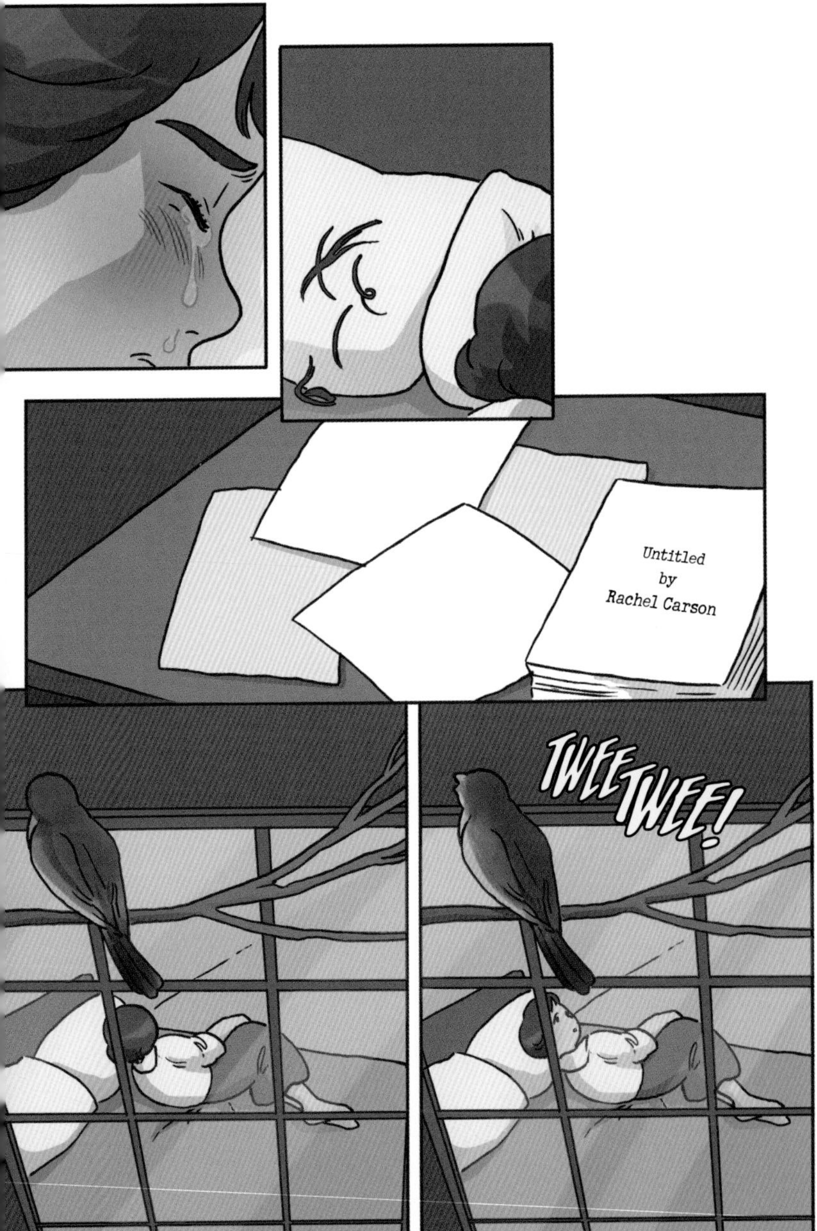
Untitled
by
Rachel Carson
TWEE TWEE!

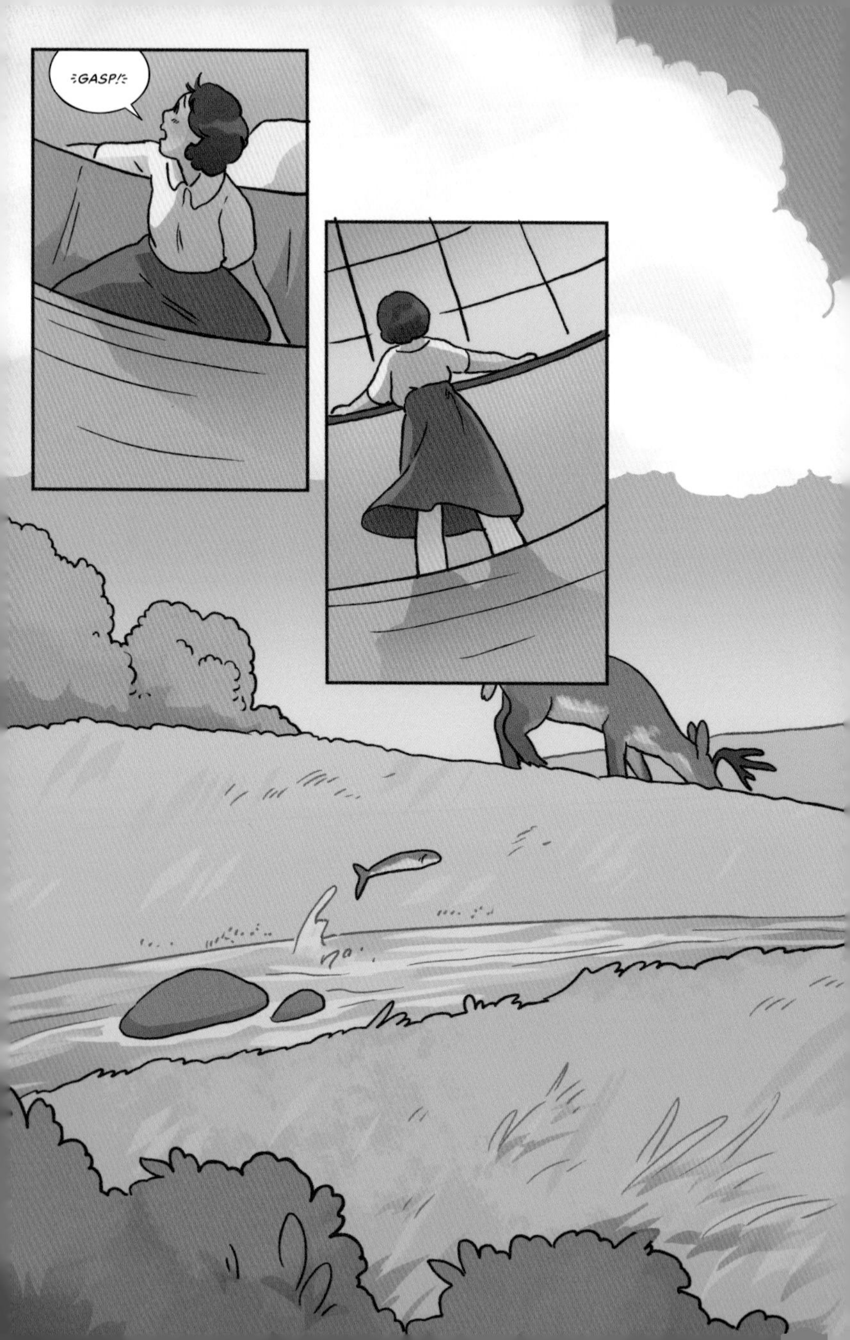
GASP!

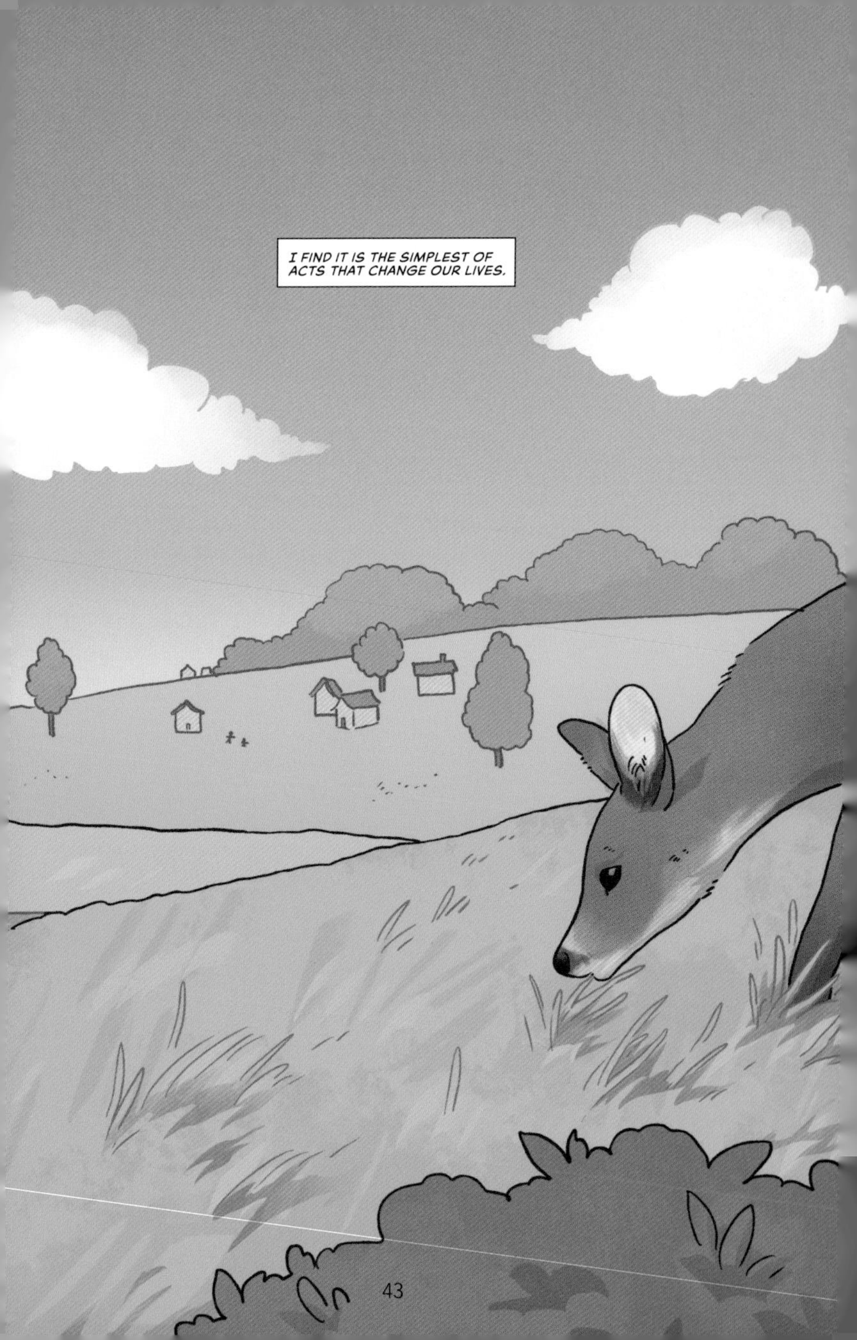
I FIND IT IS THE SIMPLEST OF ACTS THAT CHANGE OUR LIVES.

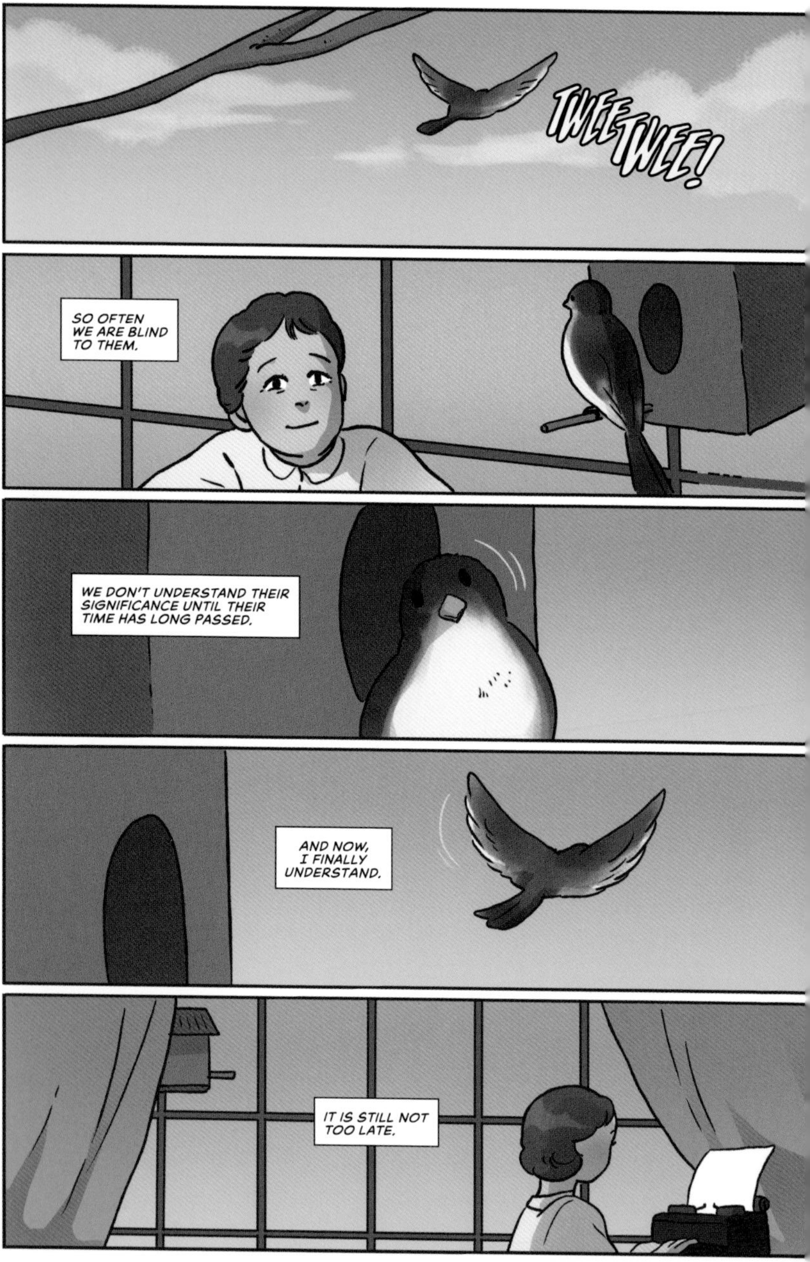
TWEE TWEE!
SO OFTEN WE ARE BLIND TO THEM.
WE DON'T UNDERSTAND THEIR SIGNIFICANCE UNTIL THEIR TIME HAS LONG PASSED.
AND NOW, I FINALLY UNDERSTAND.
IT IS STILL NOT TOO LATE.

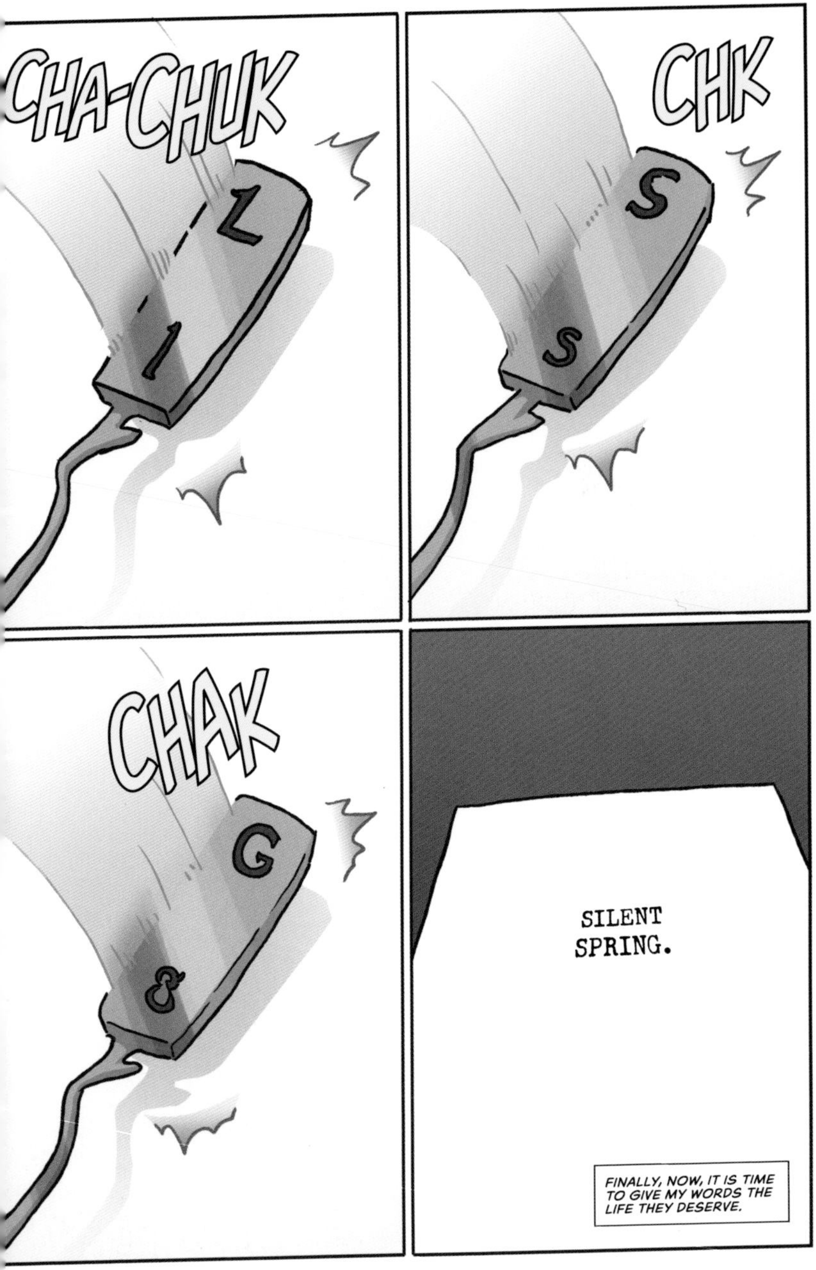
CHA-CHUK
L
I
CHK
S
S
CHAK
G
&
SILENT SPRING.
FINALLY, NOW, IT IS TIME TO GIVE MY WORDS THE LIFE THEY DESERVE.

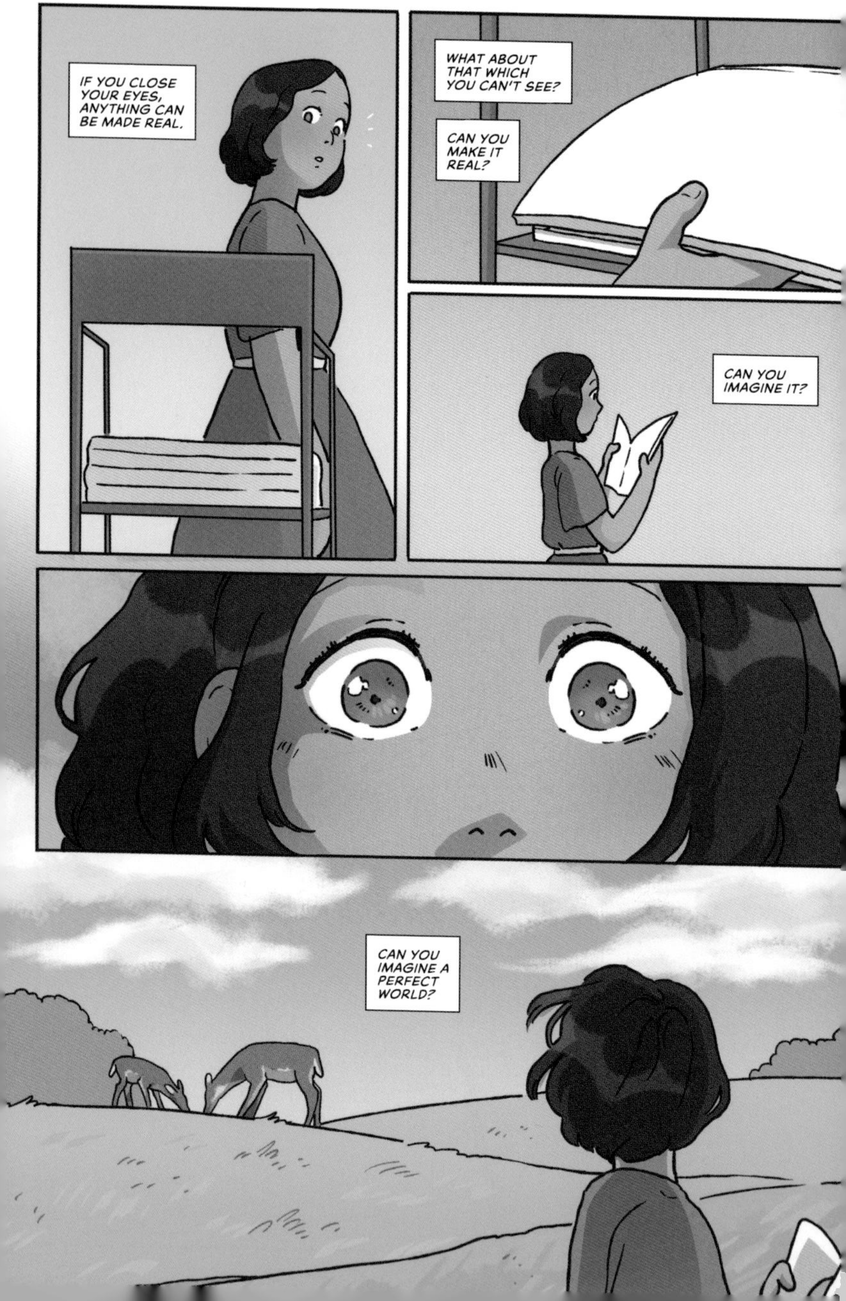
IF YOU CLOSE YOUR EYES, ANYTHING CAN BE MADE REAL.
WHAT ABOUT THAT WHICH YOU CAN'T SEE?
CAN YOU MAKE IT REAL?
CAN YOU IMAGINE IT?
CAN YOU IMAGINE A PERFECT WORLD?

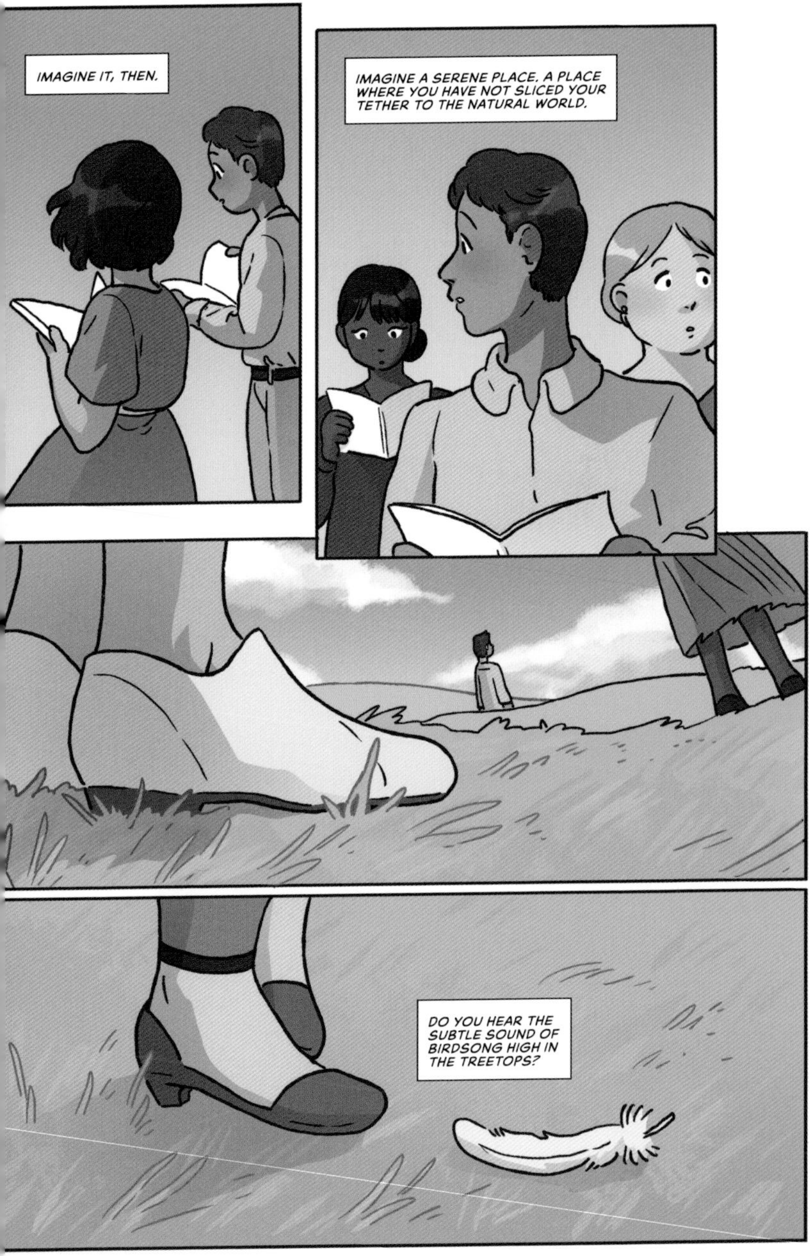
IMAGINE IT, THEN.
IMAGINE A SERENE PLACE. A PLACE WHERE YOU HAVE NOT SLICED YOUR TETHER TO THE NATURAL WORLD.
DO YOU HEAR THE SUBTLE SOUND OF BIRDSONG HIGH IN THE TREETOPS?

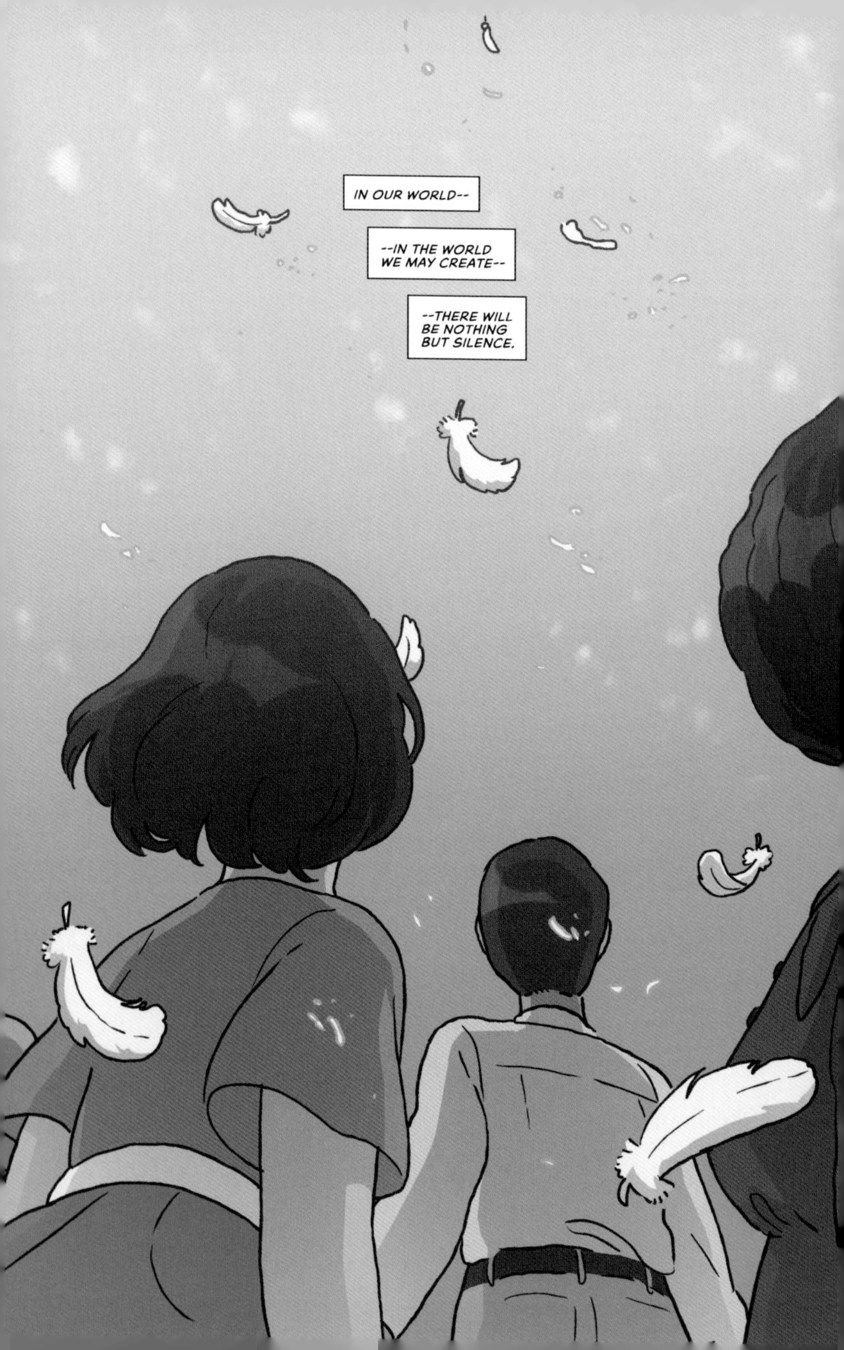
IN OUR WORLD--
--IN THE WORLD WE MAY CREATE--
--THERE WILL BE NOTHING BUT SILENCE.

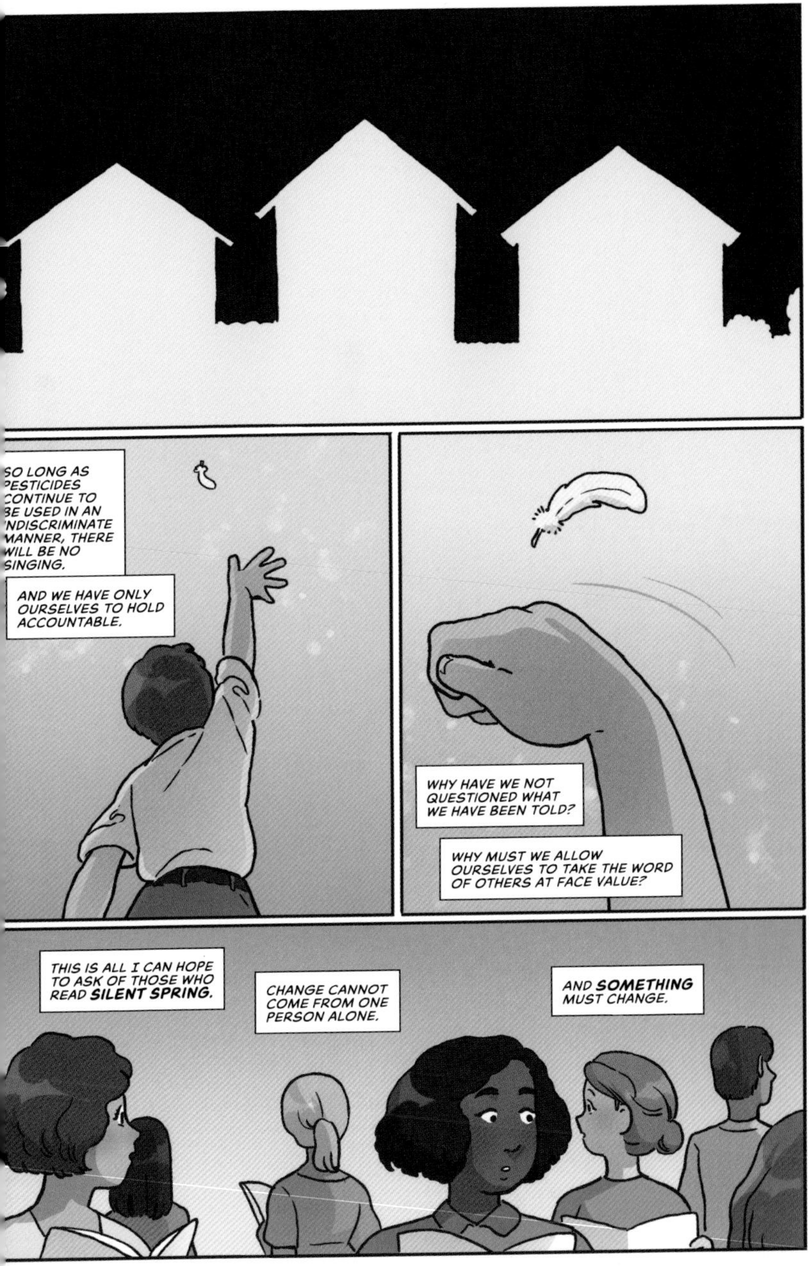
SO LONG AS PESTICIDES CONTINUE TO BE USED IN AN INDISCRIMINATE MANNER, THERE WILL BE NO SINGING.
AND WE HAVE ONLY OURSELVES TO HOLD ACCOUNTABLE.
WHY HAVE WE NOT QUESTIONED WHAT WE HAVE BEEN TOLD?
WHY MUST WE ALLOW OURSELVES TO TAKE THE WORD OF OTHERS AT FACE VALUE?
THIS IS ALL I CAN HOPE TO ASK OF THOSE WHO READ **SILENT SPRING.**
CHANGE CANNOT COME FROM ONE PERSON ALONE.
AND **SOMETHING** MUST CHANGE.

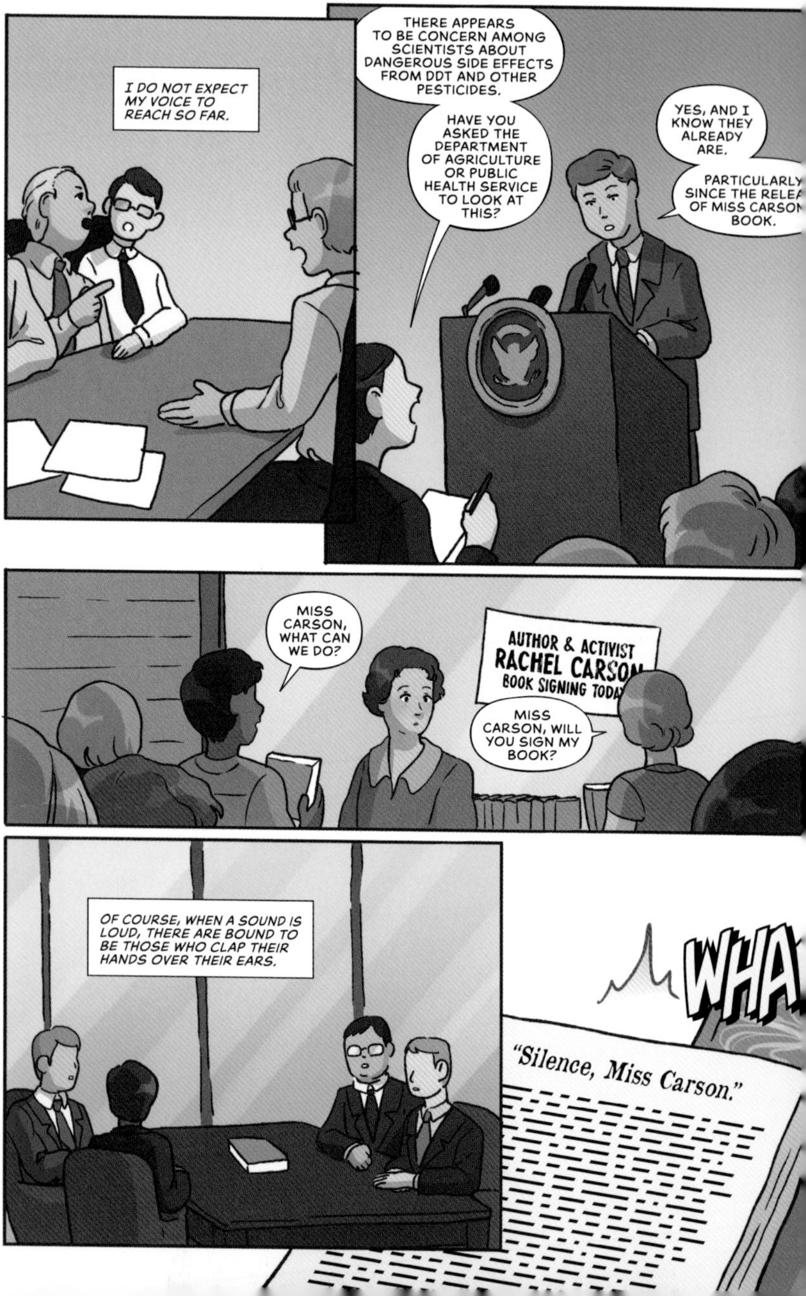
I DO NOT EXPECT MY VOICE TO REACH SO FAR.
THERE APPEARS TO BE CONCERN AMONG SCIENTISTS ABOUT DANGEROUS SIDE EFFECTS FROM DDT AND OTHER PESTICIDES.
HAVE YOU ASKED THE DEPARTMENT OF AGRICULTURE OR PUBLIC HEALTH SERVICE TO LOOK AT THIS?
YES, AND I KNOW THEY ALREADY ARE.
PARTICULARLY SINCE THE RELEA OF MISS CARSON BOOK.
MISS CARSON, WHAT CAN WE DO?
AUTHOR & ACTIVIST
RACHEL CARSO
BOOK SIGNING TODA
MISS CARSON, WILL YOU SIGN MY BOOK?
OF COURSE, WHEN A SOUND IS LOUD, THERE ARE BOUND TO BE THOSE WHO CLAP THEIR HANDS OVER THEIR EARS.
WHA
"Silence, Miss Carson."

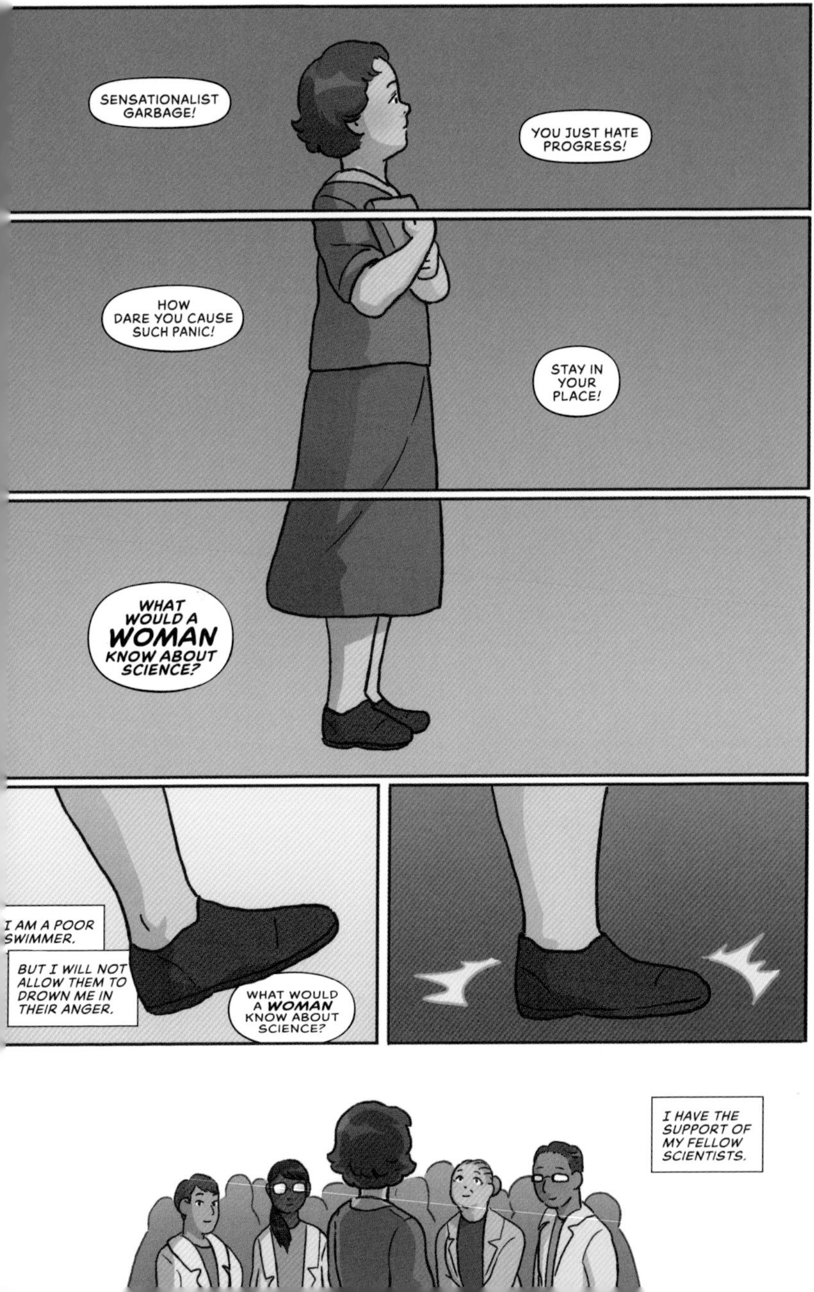
SENSATIONALIST GARBAGE!
YOU JUST HATE PROGRESS!
HOW DARE YOU CAUSE SUCH PANIC!
STAY IN YOUR PLACE!
WHAT WOULD A WOMAN KNOW ABOUT SCIENCE?
I AM A POOR SWIMMER.
BUT I WILL NOT ALLOW THEM TO DROWN ME IN THEIR ANGER.
WHAT WOULD A WOMAN KNOW ABOUT SCIENCE?
I HAVE THE SUPPORT OF MY FELLOW SCIENTISTS.

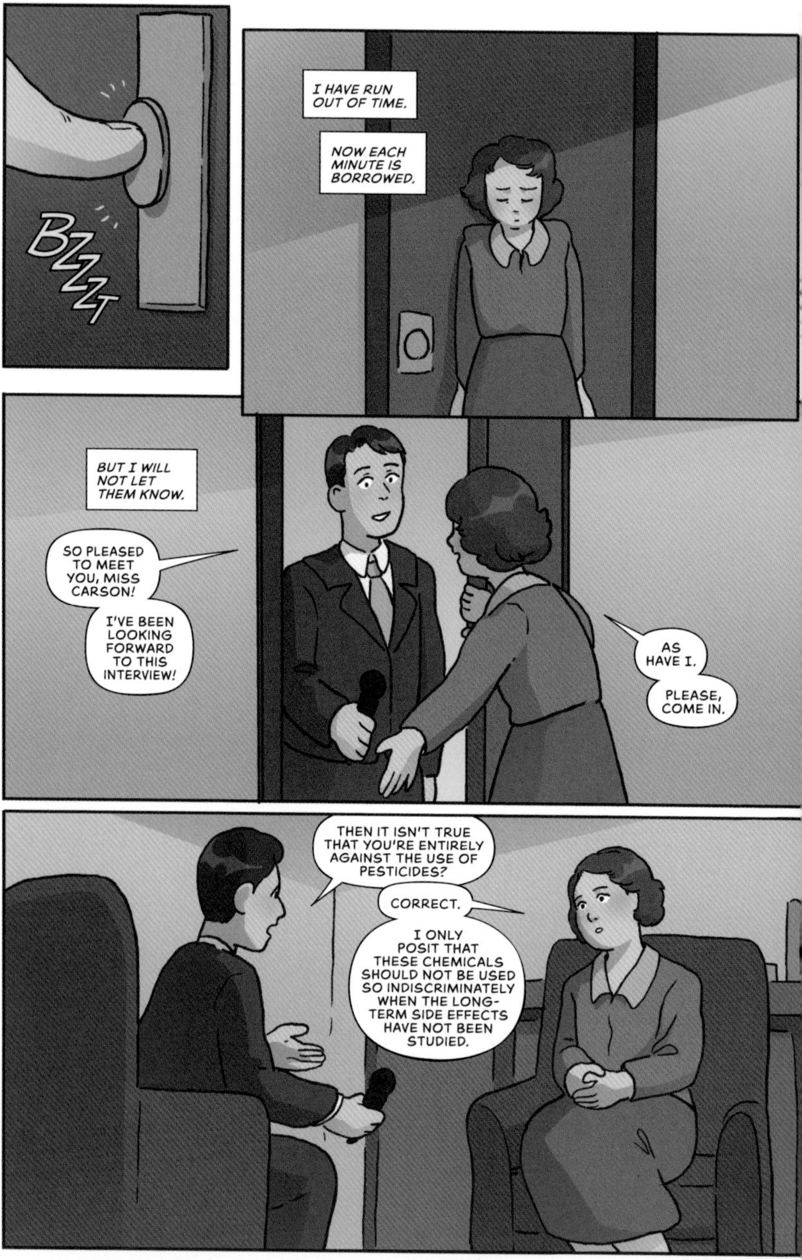
BZZZT
I HAVE RUN OUT OF TIME.
NOW EACH MINUTE IS BORROWED.
BUT I WILL NOT LET THEM KNOW.
SO PLEASED TO MEET YOU, MISS CARSON!
I'VE BEEN LOOKING FORWARD TO THIS INTERVIEW!
AS HAVE I.
PLEASE, COME IN.
THEN IT ISN'T TRUE THAT YOU'RE ENTIRELY AGAINST THE USE OF PESTICIDES?
CORRECT.
I ONLY POSIT THAT THESE CHEMICALS SHOULD NOT BE USED SO INDISCRIMINATELY WHEN THE LONG-TERM SIDE EFFECTS HAVE NOT BEEN STUDIED.

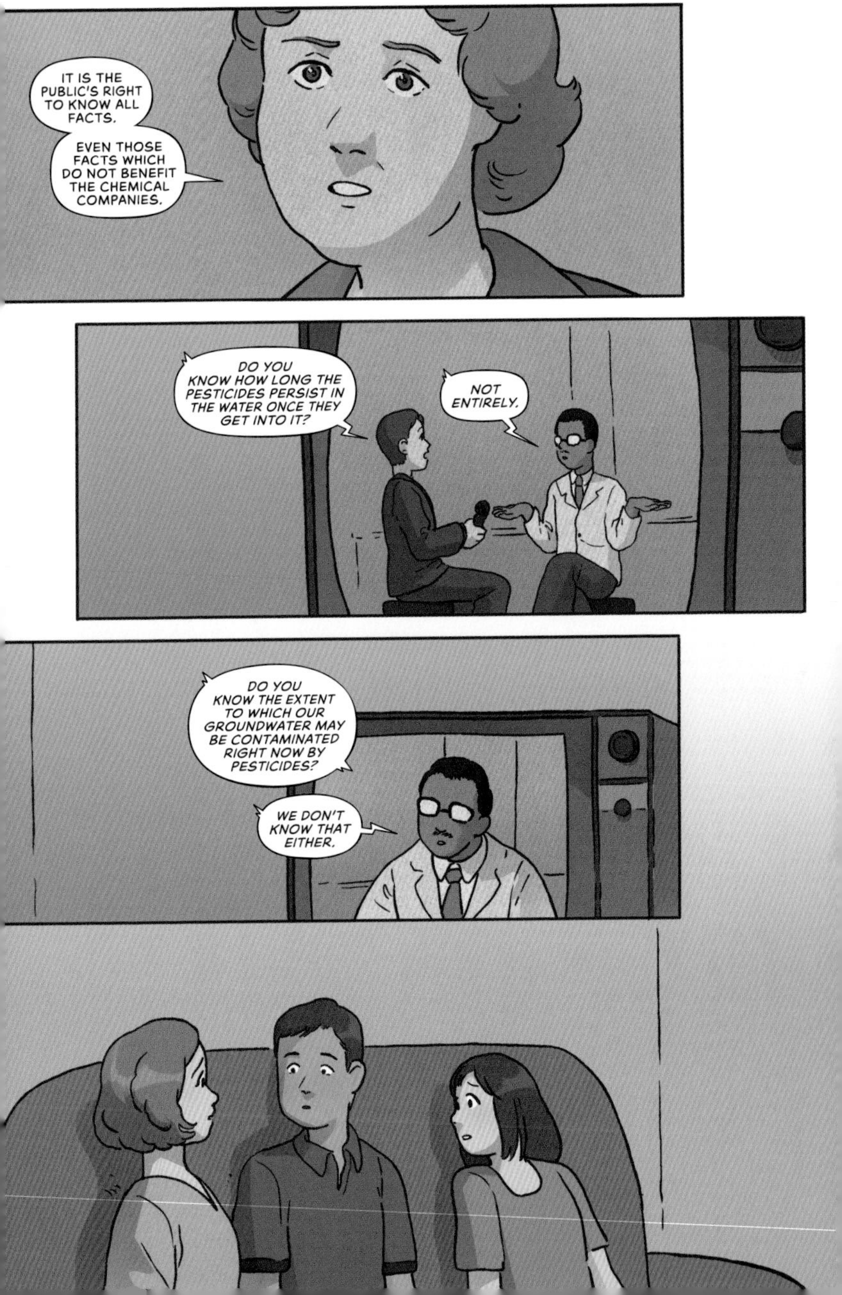
IT IS THE PUBLIC'S RIGHT TO KNOW ALL FACTS.
EVEN THOSE FACTS WHICH DO NOT BENEFIT THE CHEMICAL COMPANIES.
DO YOU KNOW HOW LONG THE PESTICIDES PERSIST IN THE WATER ONCE THEY GET INTO IT?
NOT ENTIRELY.
DO YOU KNOW THE EXTENT TO WHICH OUR GROUNDWATER MAY BE CONTAMINATED RIGHT NOW BY PESTICIDES?
WE DON'T KNOW THAT EITHER.

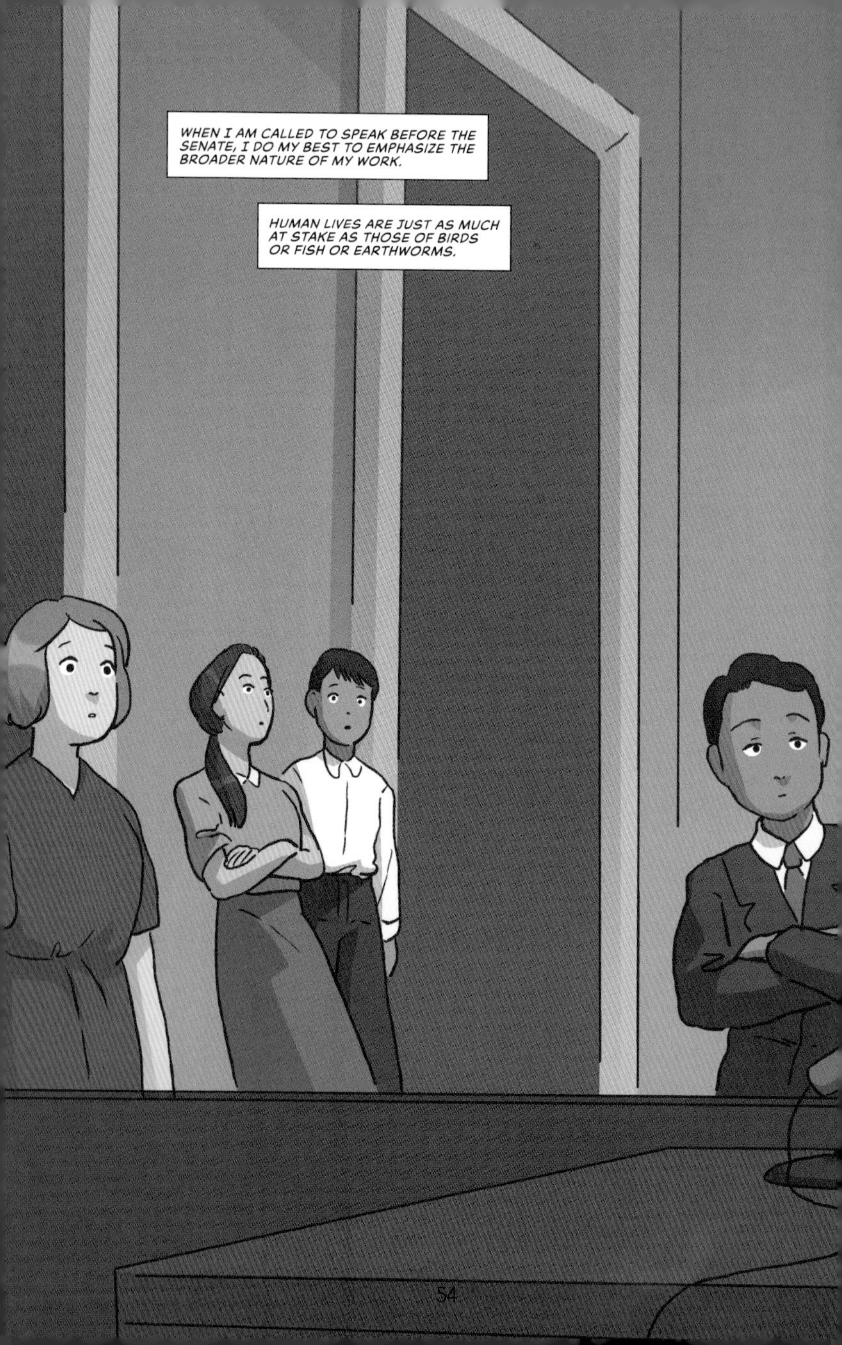
WHEN I AM CALLED TO SPEAK BEFORE THE SENATE, I DO MY BEST TO EMPHASIZE THE BROADER NATURE OF MY WORK.
HUMAN LIVES ARE JUST AS MUCH AT STAKE AS THOSE OF BIRDS OR FISH OR EARTHWORMS.

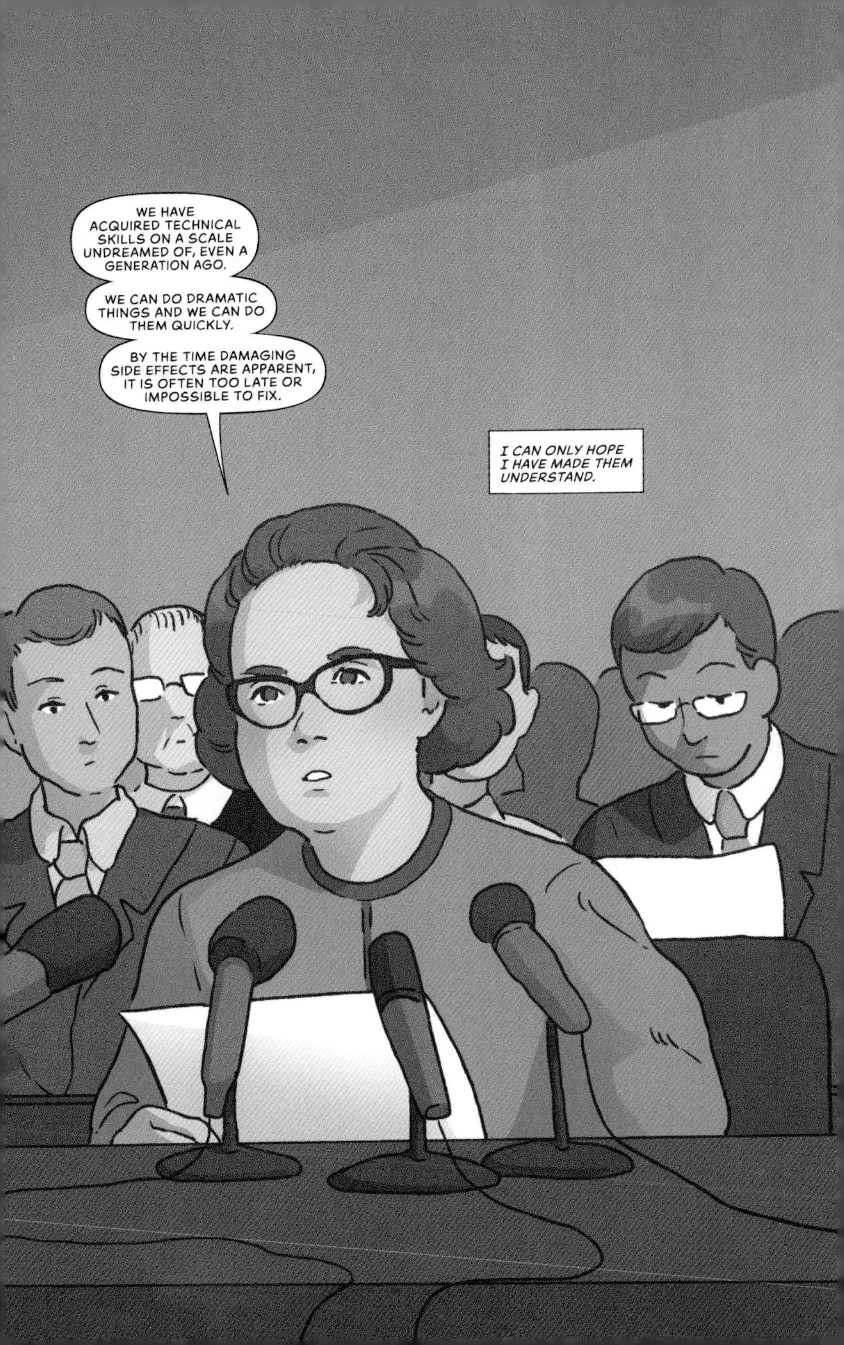
WE HAVE ACQUIRED TECHNICAL SKILLS ON A SCALE UNDREAMED OF, EVEN A GENERATION AGO.
WE CAN DO DRAMATIC THINGS AND WE CAN DO THEM QUICKLY.
BY THE TIME DAMAGING SIDE EFFECTS ARE APPARENT, IT IS OFTEN TOO LATE OR IMPOSSIBLE TO FIX.
I CAN ONLY HOPE I HAVE MADE THEM UNDERSTAND.

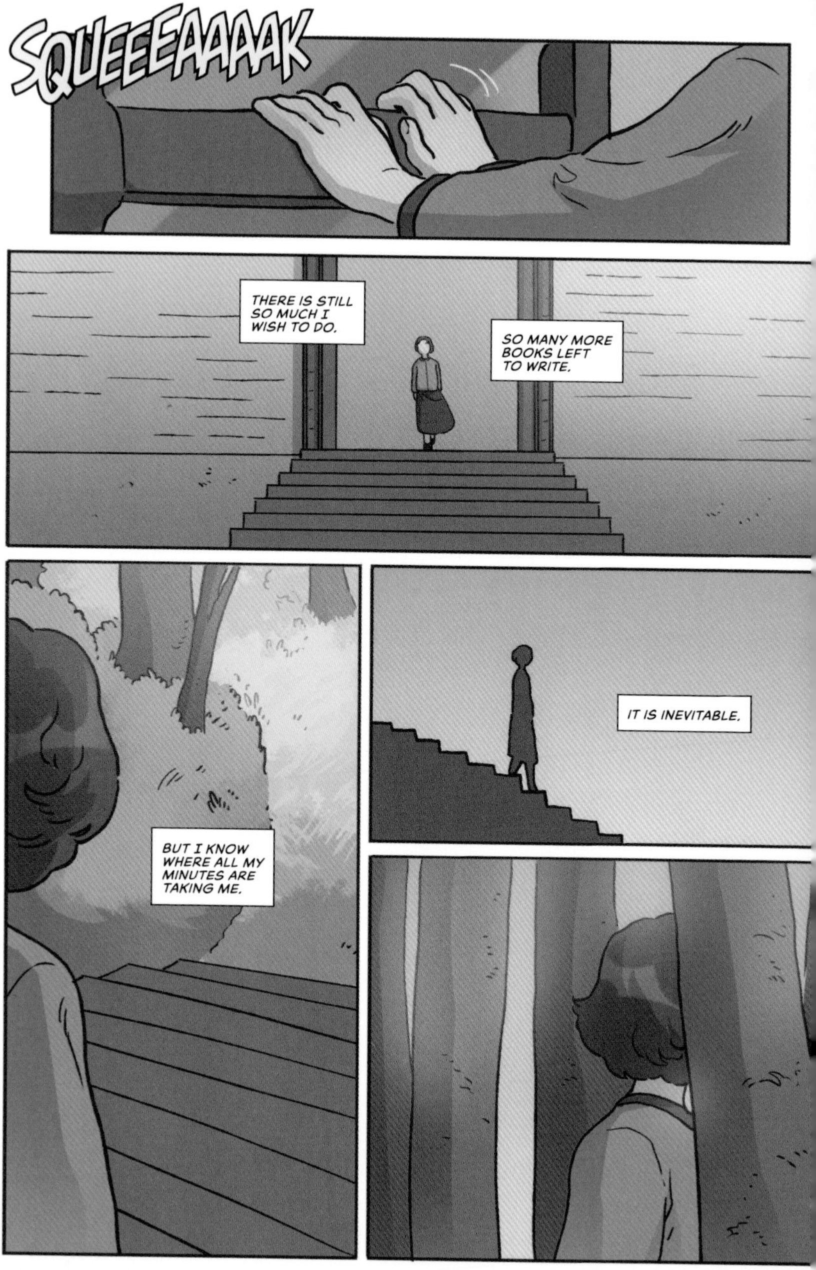
SQUEEEAAAAK
THERE IS STILL SO MUCH I WISH TO DO.
SO MANY MORE BOOKS LEFT TO WRITE.
IT IS INEVITABLE.
BUT I KNOW WHERE ALL MY MINUTES ARE TAKING ME.

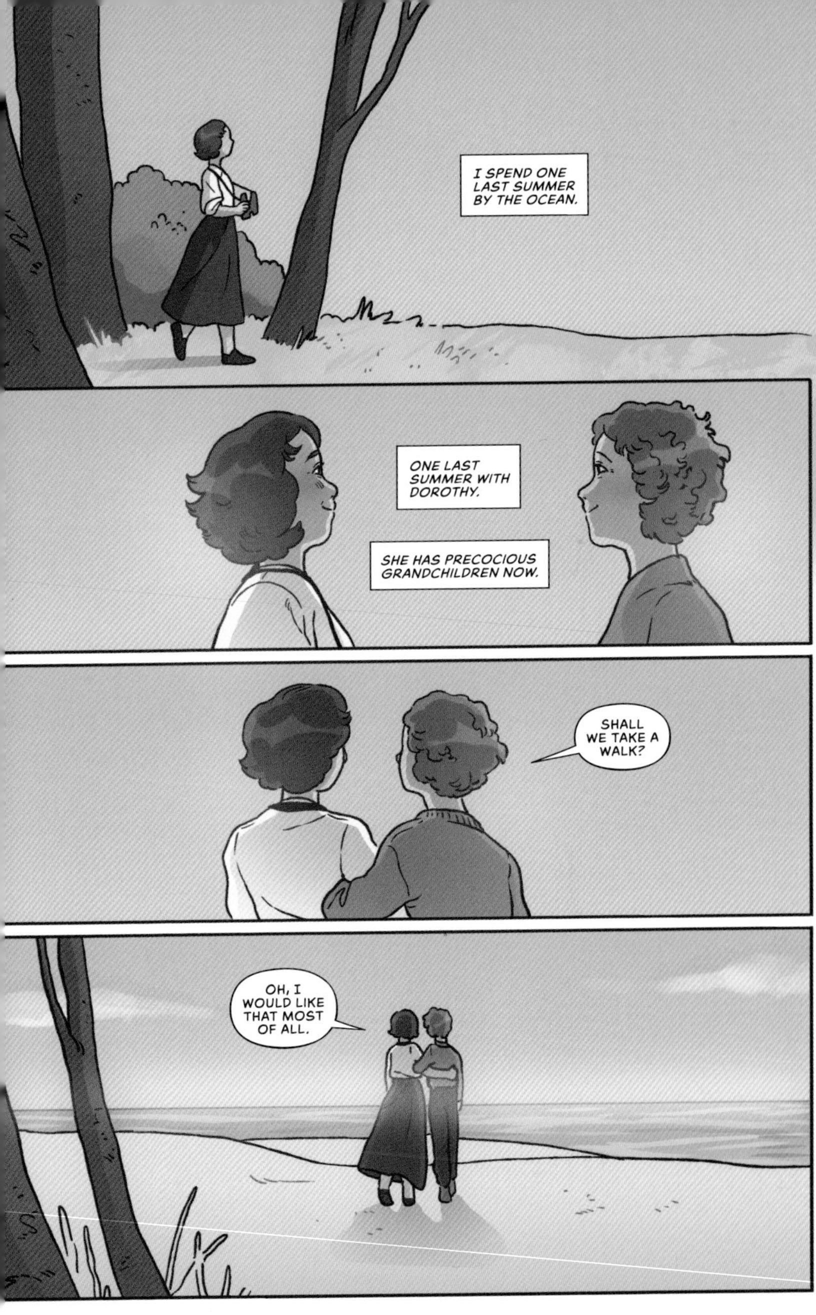
I SPEND ONE LAST SUMMER BY THE OCEAN.
ONE LAST SUMMER WITH DOROTHY.
SHE HAS PRECOCIOUS GRANDCHILDREN NOW.
SHALL WE TAKE A WALK?
OH, I WOULD LIKE THAT MOST OF ALL.

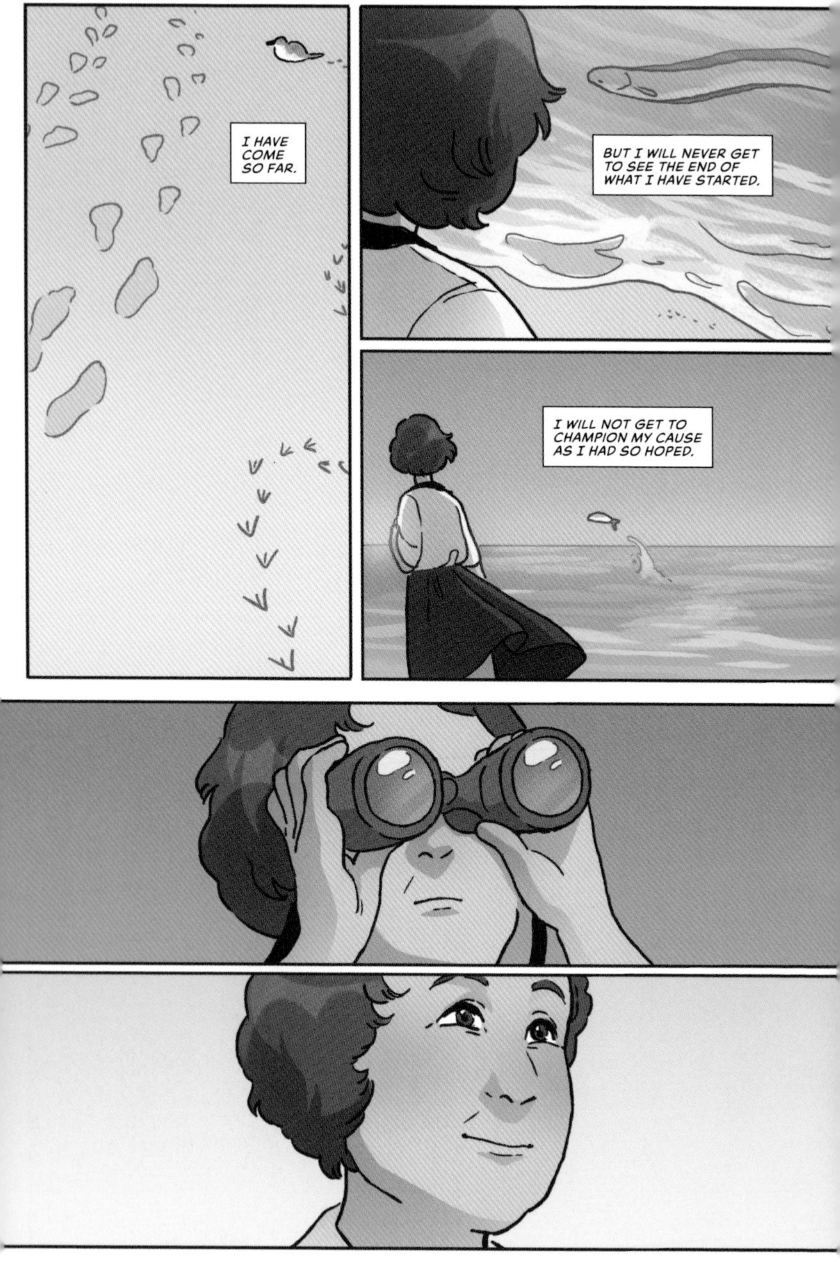
I HAVE COME SO FAR.
BUT I WILL NEVER GET TO SEE THE END OF WHAT I HAVE STARTED.
I WILL NOT GET TO CHAMPION MY CAUSE AS I HAD SO HOPED.

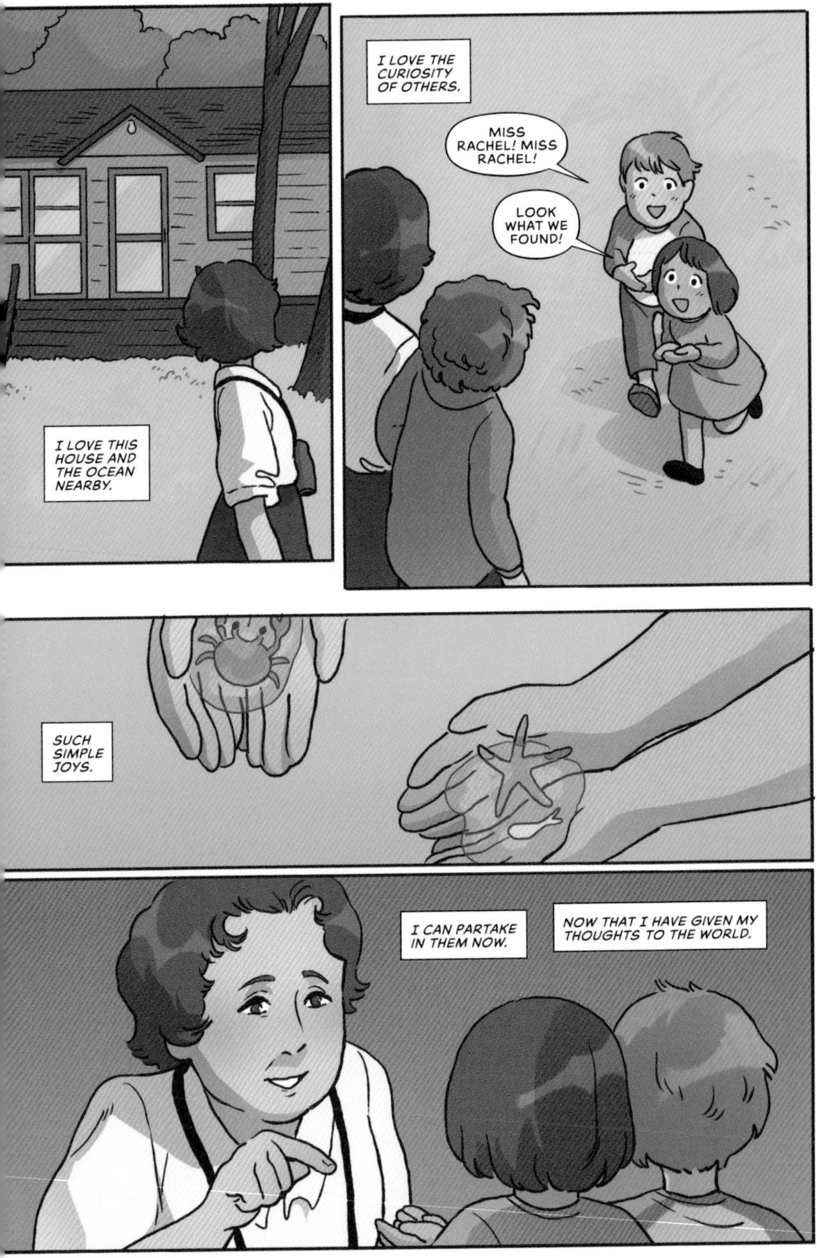
I LOVE THIS HOUSE AND THE OCEAN NEARBY.
I LOVE THE CURIOSITY OF OTHERS.
MISS RACHEL! MISS RACHEL!
LOOK WHAT WE FOUND!
SUCH SIMPLE JOYS.
I CAN PARTAKE IN THEM NOW.
NOW THAT I HAVE GIVEN MY THOUGHTS TO THE WORLD.

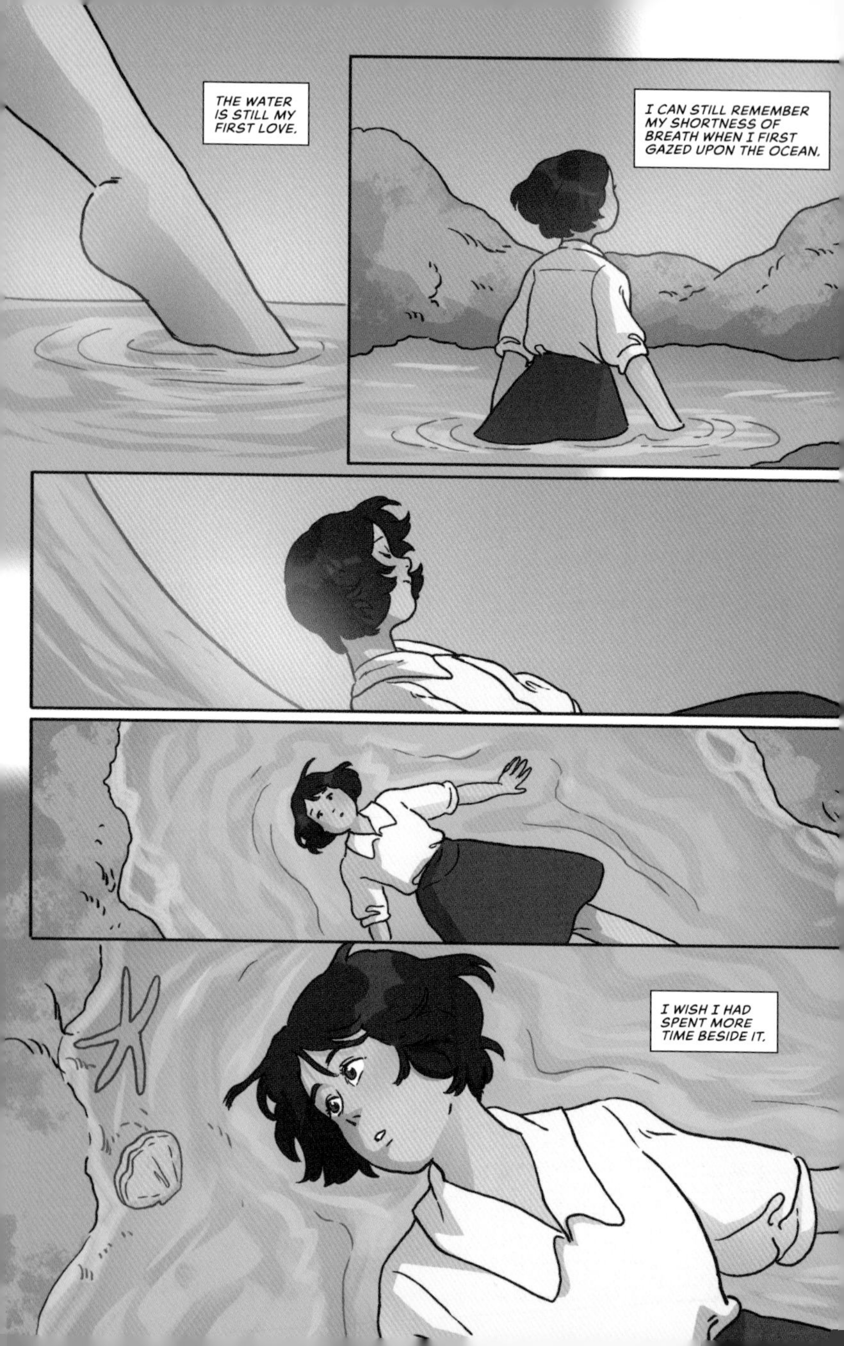
THE WATER IS STILL MY FIRST LOVE.
I CAN STILL REMEMBER MY SHORTNESS OF BREATH WHEN I FIRST GAZED UPON THE OCEAN.
I WISH I HAD SPENT MORE TIME BESIDE IT.

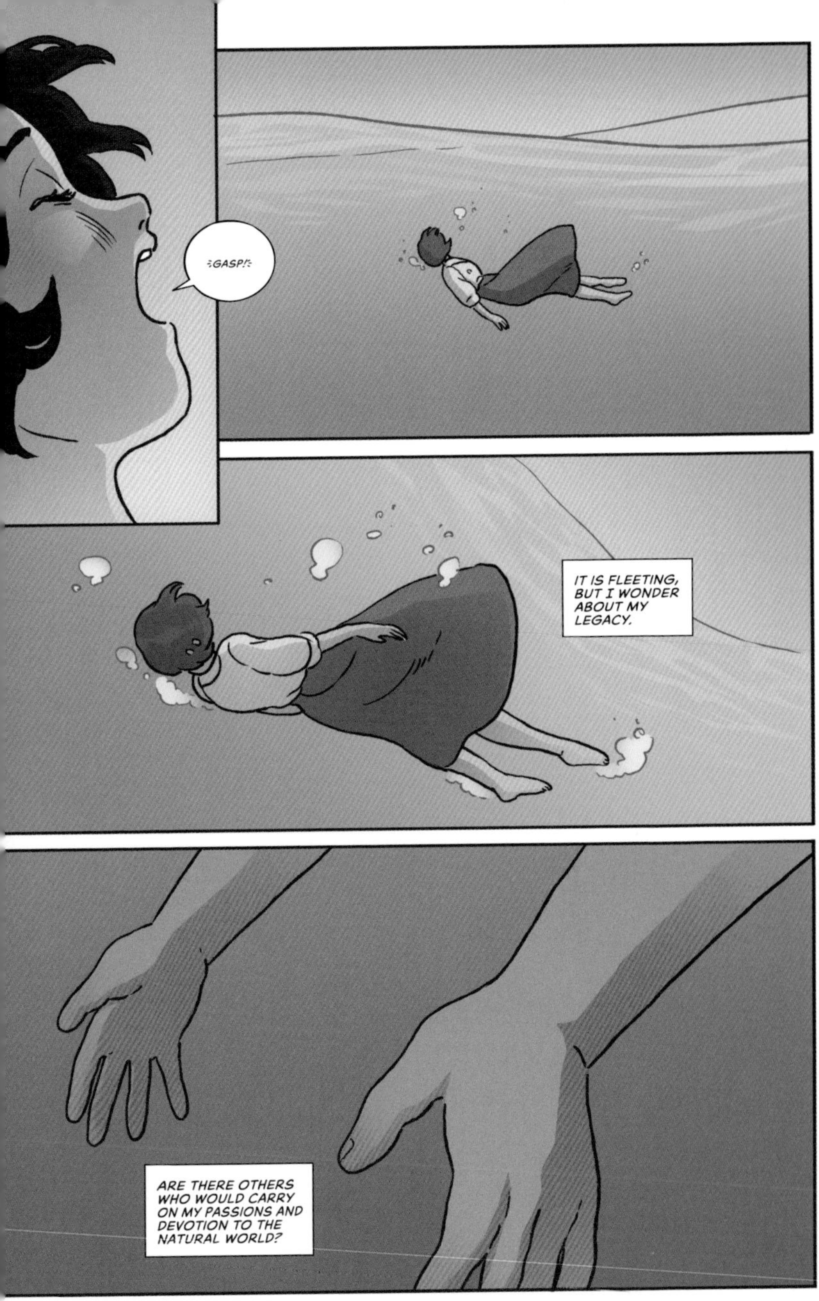

:GASP!:
IT IS FLEETING, BUT I WONDER ABOUT MY LEGACY.
ARE THERE OTHERS WHO WOULD CARRY ON MY PASSIONS AND DEVOTION TO THE NATURAL WORLD?

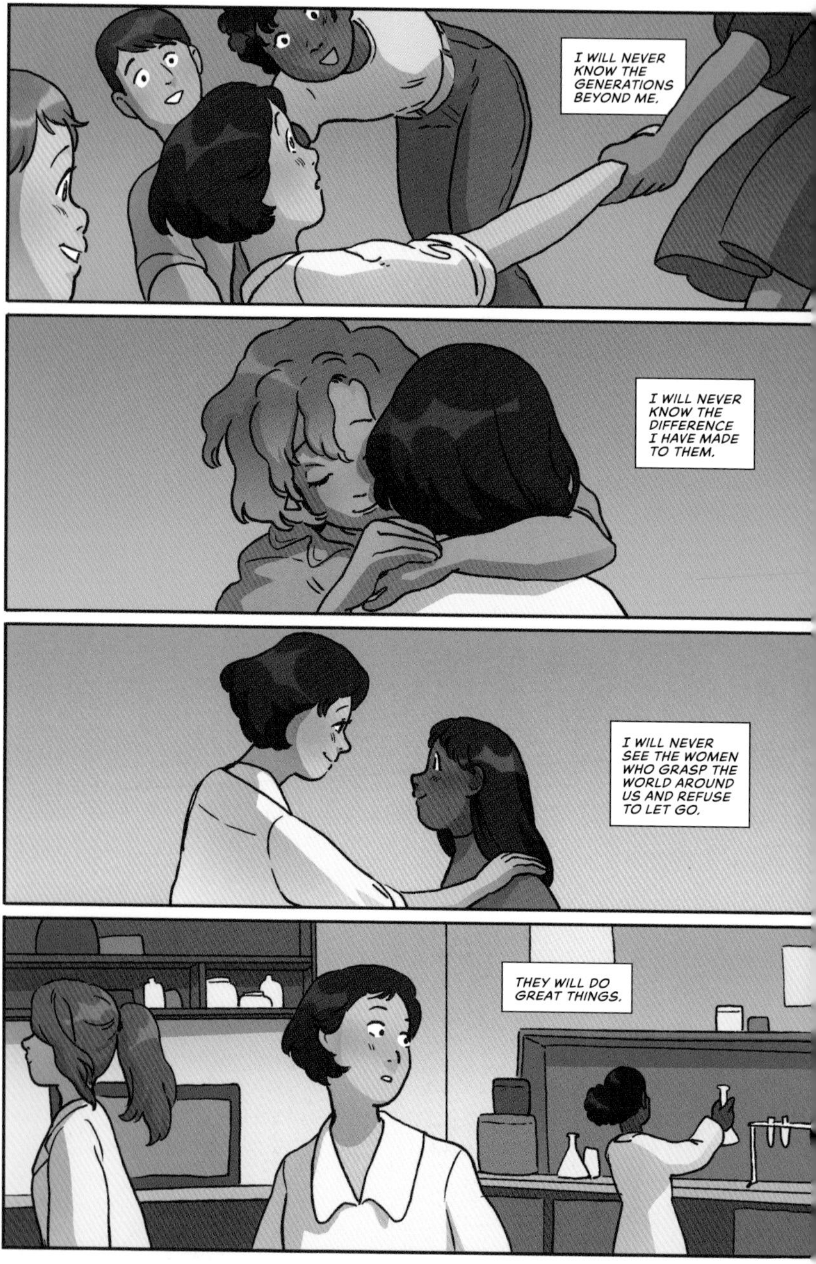
I WILL NEVER KNOW THE GENERATIONS BEYOND ME.
I WILL NEVER KNOW THE DIFFERENCE I HAVE MADE TO THEM.
I WILL NEVER SEE THE WOMEN WHO GRASP THE WORLD AROUND US AND REFUSE TO LET GO.
THEY WILL DO GREAT THINGS.

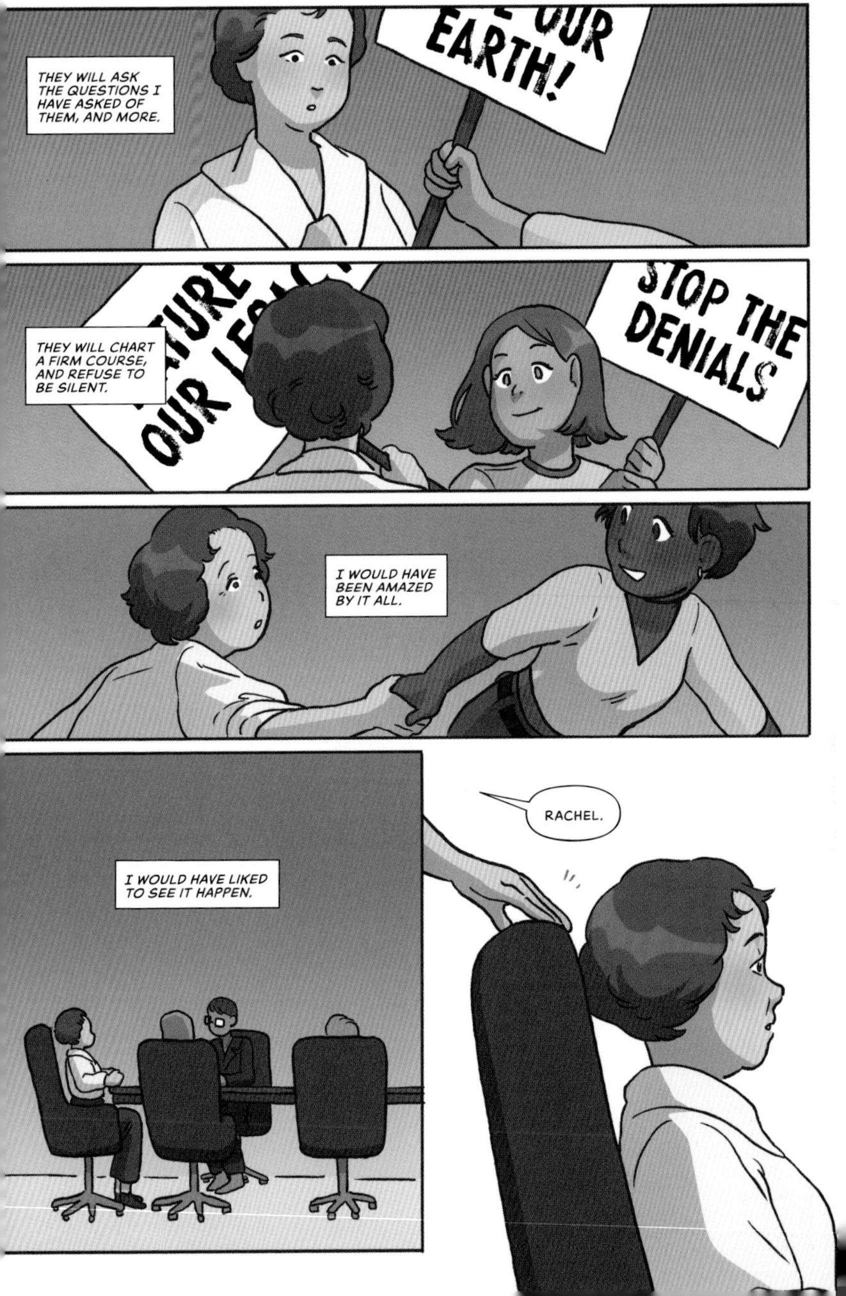
THEY WILL ASK THE QUESTIONS I HAVE ASKED OF THEM, AND MORE.
EARTH!
THEY WILL CHART A FIRM COURSE, AND REFUSE TO BE SILENT.
STOP THE DENIALS
I WOULD HAVE BEEN AMAZED BY IT ALL.
I WOULD HAVE LIKED TO SEE IT HAPPEN.
RACHEL.

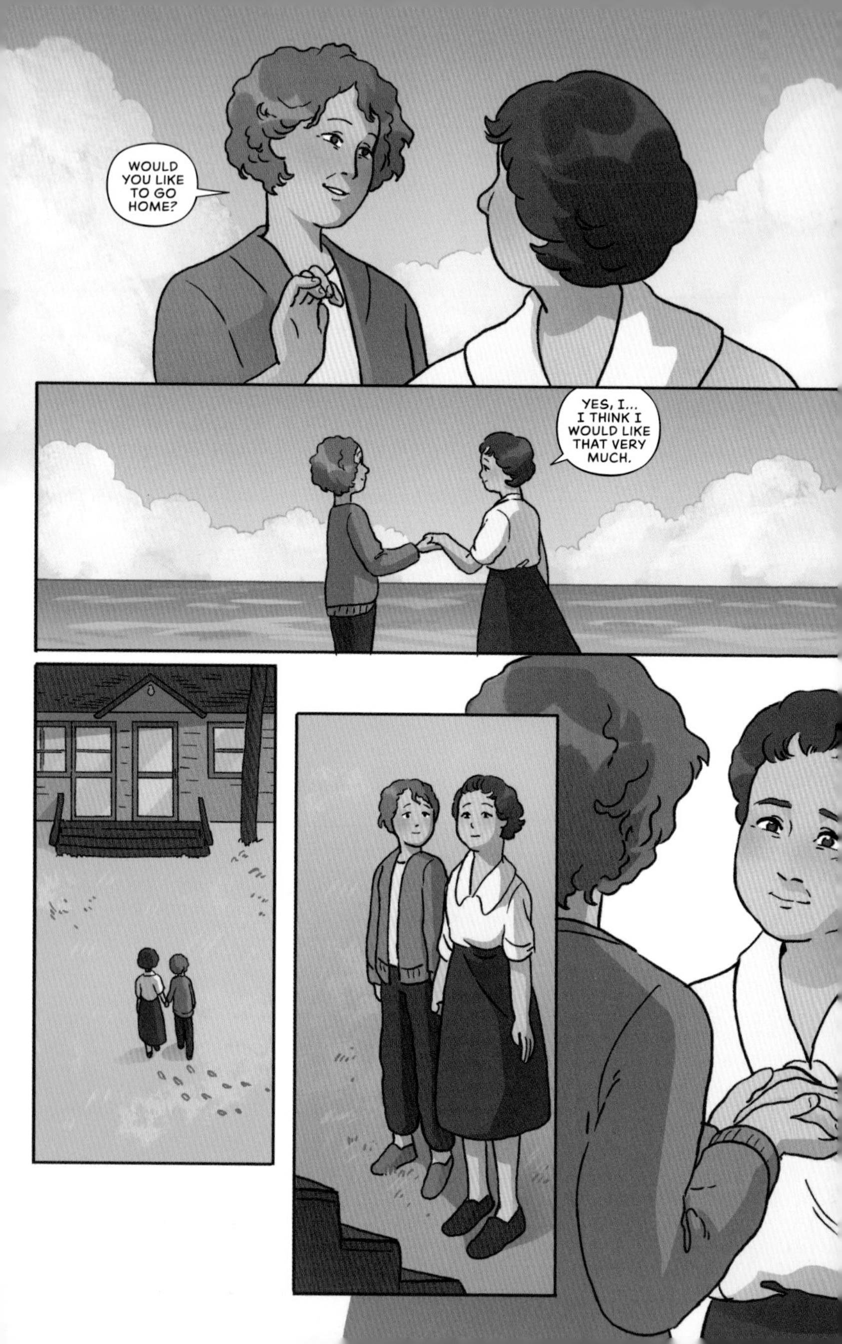
WOULD YOU LIKE TO GO HOME?
YES, I... I THINK I WOULD LIKE THAT VERY MUCH.

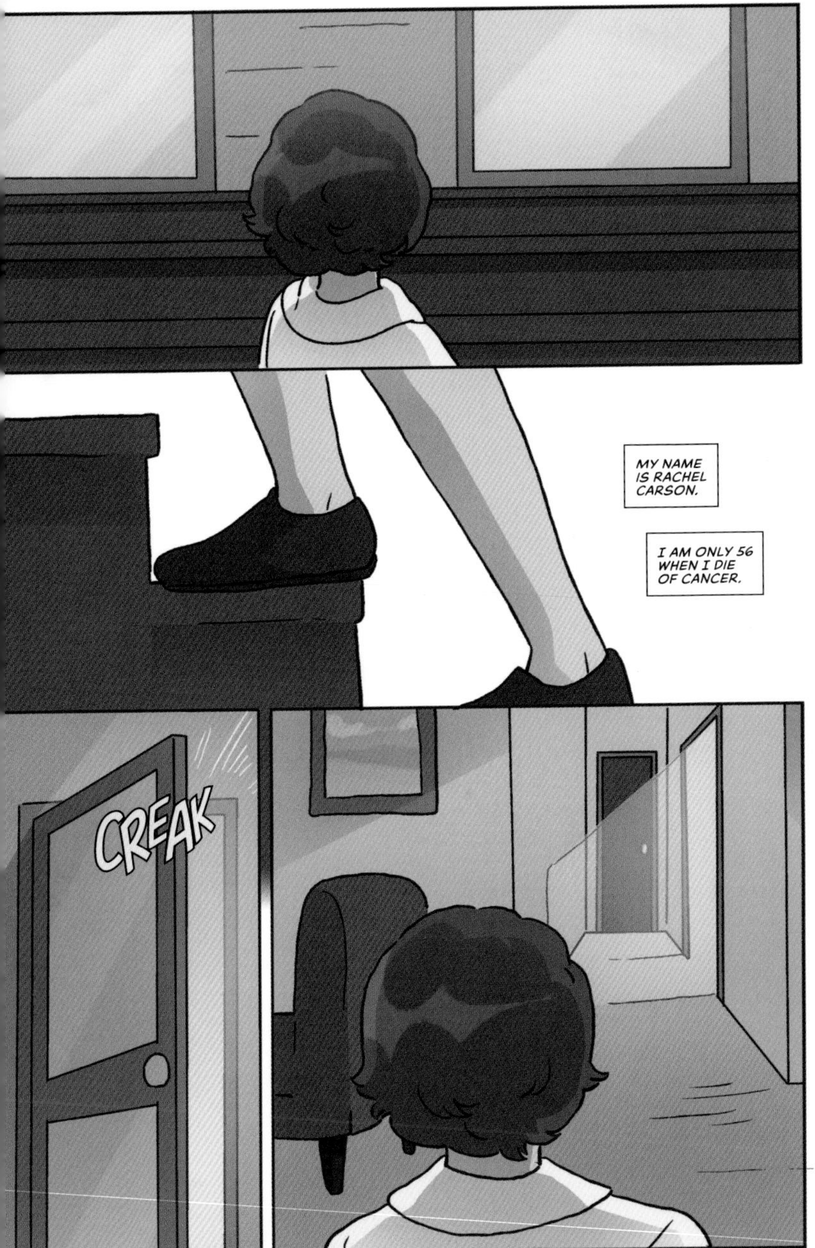
MY NAME IS RACHEL CARSON.
I AM ONLY 56 WHEN I DIE OF CANCER.
CREAK

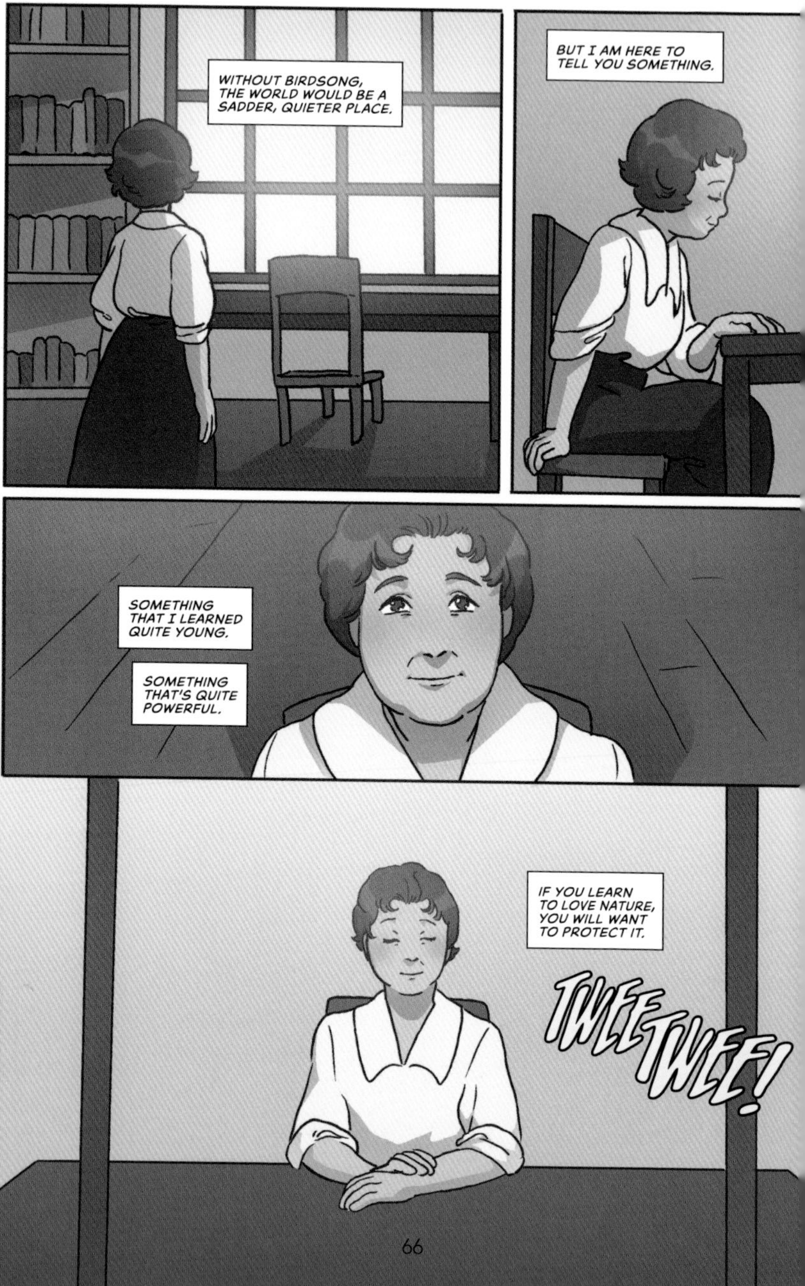
WITHOUT BIRDSONG, THE WORLD WOULD BE A SADDER, QUIETER PLACE.
BUT I AM HERE TO TELL YOU SOMETHING.
SOMETHING THAT I LEARNED QUITE YOUNG.
SOMETHING THAT'S QUITE POWERFUL.
IF YOU LEARN TO LOVE NATURE, YOU WILL WANT TO PROTECT IT.
TWEE TWEE!

BIBLIOGRAPHY

1. Carlisle, David L.H. "Rachel Carson's Early Life." Rachel Carson Homestead: Springdale, PA, 16 Nov 2019.

2. Carson, Rachel. *Silent Spring*. Penguin Books, in Association with Hamish Hamilton, 2015.

3. Carson, Rachel, with an Introduction by Brian Vesey-Fitzgerald. *The Sea: The Sea Around Us, Under the Sea-Wind, The Edge of the Sea*. Paladin, 1991.

4. Lear, Linda. "The Life and Legacy of Rachel Carson." *RachelCarson.org*, 2020. www.rachelcarson.org/.

5. Lear, Linda. *Rachel Carson: Witness for Nature*. Mariner Books, 2009.

6. "Rachel Carson." *American Experience*, Written and Directed by Michelle Ferrari, Season 29, episode 4, PBS, 19 May 2018. https://www.pbs.org/wgbh/americanexperience/films/rachel-carson.

7. Souder, William. *On a Farther Shore: The Life and Legacy of Rachel Carson, Author of Silent Spring*. Broadway Books, 2013.

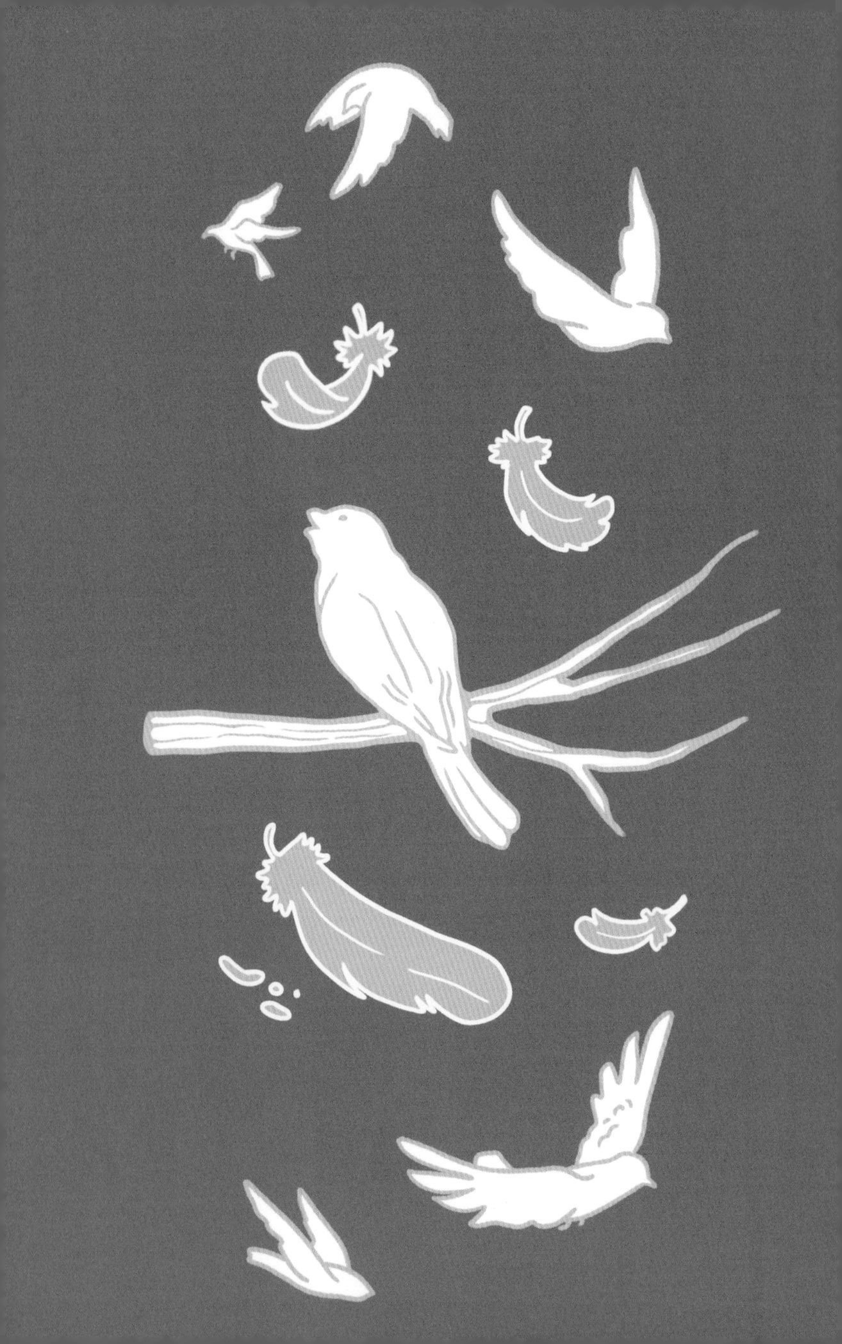

SEEN™
—Rachel Carson—
TEACHING GUIDE

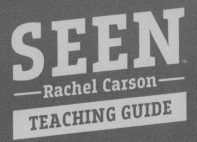

Learning Standards

The questions and activities in this teacher guide correlate with the following Common Core English Language Arts Standards (www.corestandards.org) for Grades 6, 7-10, and 9-10:

ELA Reading: Literature Standards
- Key Ideas and Details RL.6-10.1, RL.6-10.2, RL.6-10.3;
- Craft and Structure RL.6-10.4, RL.6-10.5, RL.6-10.6;
- Integration of Knowledge and Ideas RL9-10.7.

ELA Reading: Informational Texts Standards
- Key Ideas and Details RI.6-10.1, RI.6-10.2, RI.6-10.3;
- Craft and Structure RI.6-10.4, RI.6-10.5, RI.6-10.6;
- Integration of Knowledge and Ideas RI.6-10.7, RI.6-10.8.

ELA Writing Standards
- Text Types and Purposes W.6-10.1, W.6-10.2, W.6-10.3;
- Production and Distribution of Writing W.6-10.4, W.6-10.5, W.6-10.6;
- Research to Build and Present Knowledge W.6-10.7, W.6-10.8, W.6-10.9.

ELA Speaking and Listening Standards
- Comprehension and Collaboration SL.6-10.1, SL.6-10.2, SL.6-10.3;
- Presentation of Knowledge and Ideas SL.6-10.4, SL.6-10.5, SL.6-10.6.

ELA History/Social Studies Standards
- Key Ideas and Details RH.6-8.1;
- Craft and Structure RH.6-8.4, RH.6-8.5, RH.6-8.6;
- Integration of Knowledge and Ideas RH.6-8.8

Next Generation Science Standards: Earth and Human Activity
- Human Impacts on Earth Systems ESS3.C
- Cause and Effect MS-ESS3-2

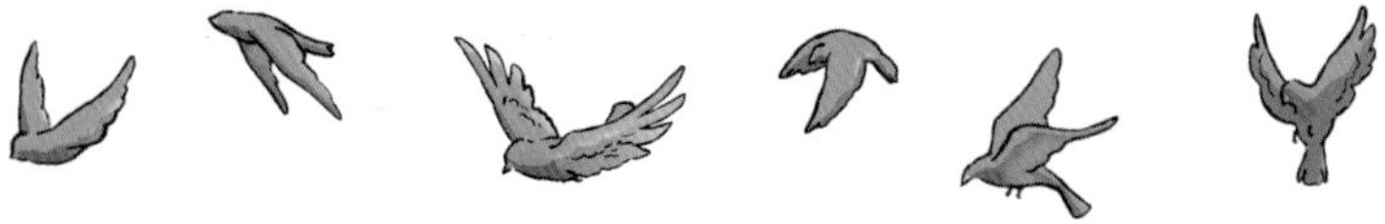

A General Approach

It is highly recommended that you read Scott McCloud's *Understanding Comics*[1], specifically pages 60-63, which deal with closure; pages 70-72, which deal with panel transitions; and 152-155, which deal with word/picture combinations. Depending on the needs of your class, you can have students learn these specific terms and use them to identify the different transition and combination styles. Alternatively, you can utilize your understanding of them to guide discussion, when examining specific panels or pages.

Highlight individual panels and or pages, and ask the following questions:

- What is going on in this panel or on this page?
- What is the purpose of the specific pictures in telling the story? How do they enhance the words?
- Why did the creator choose to put these words and pictures together in this way?
- How does color affect the scene?
- What do we learn about the character from the images?
- What mood is being set and how?

Examine the specific sequence of panels:

- Why did the creator put these panels in this particular order?
- What's happening between the panels?
- How does the transition between these panels indicate things like mood and character?
- How do the panel transitions affect the speed of the scene?
- Why did the creator choose this speed?

LET'S GET ACTIVE!

A great exercise is to have students act out a short scene in the book, getting them to fill in the action occurring between the panels. This demonstrates to them that the gutter (that space between panels) is just as important as the other storytelling elements in the book.

1. *McCloud, Scott, 1960-. Understanding Comics: the Invisible Art. New York: HarperPerennial, 1994.*

Pre-Reading Activities

- What does the cover tell you about the story? Does it make you want to read the book? Why or why not?

- Rachel Carson lived from 1907 to 1964. How common was it for women to be scientists then? How common is it now?

- What is the purpose of pesticides? What sort of pesticides are used today? Are they a good or a bad thing?

Discussion Questions

Questions about specific pages:

1. Page 9 is a splash page. What is the purpose of a splash page in a comic? What is the purpose of this one?

2. What is the purpose of the extreme close-up panel on page 11, panel 4?

3. Look at the last panel of page 13. Why is it not three separate panels? What is its effect?

4. "Time shifts its sands above land as well." (page 16) What do you think this means?

5. What is the mood on page 20? How is that mood created?

6. On page 28, panel 4, why is the font size of "Thank you" so small?

7. What has happened on pages 32-33? What is the overall feeling? How do you know?

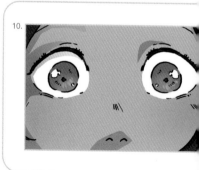

8. Examine the layout and imagery of page 38. What is being conveyed here?

9. On the bottom of page 39, why are the people shown only as outlines?

10. On page 46, what is the effect of the close-up on the girl's eyes?

11. On page 51, why is the image broken into separate panels? Do you think it suits the narration? What do you think of the narration itself?

12. What is the imagery being used on page 58? What is the effect?

13. Is the action on page 61 actually happening, or is it a feeling she's having? What is the feeling overall?

General Questions:

1. Find and cite different examples of facial expressions used to indicate the following emotions. What are some of the characteristics of the different expressions?

- Happiness
- Anger
- Sadness

- Frustration
- Shock
- Excitement

- Disappointment
- Pain

2. Rachel loves the sound of birdsong. What sounds mean something to you? What sort of sounds inspire happiness or sadness?

3. How did events like the Great Depression and World War II affect Rachel's life and career? Is there a similar worldwide event that you've experienced? How did it affect your life?

4. On page 23, the discoverer of DDT is mentioned but not named. Why do you think he isn't named? Do you think he deserved to win a Nobel Prize?

5. On page 27, Rachel says she has not learned to be cautious. Why would she say this? Should she have been more cautious? What did not being cautious do for her?

6. What is the relationship between Dorothy Freeman and Rachel Carson? Is there something deeper implied? How is this shown? Why do you think it is only implied?

7. Why does Rachel conceal her illness? How does Rachel overcome her illness and move forward?

2.

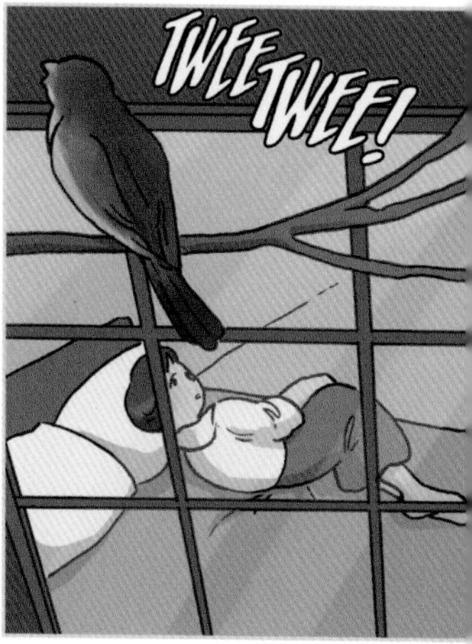
TWEE TWEE!

6.

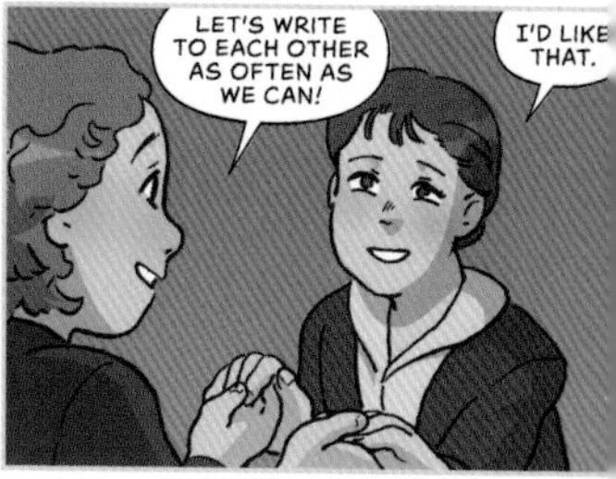
LET'S WRITE TO EACH OTHER AS OFTEN AS WE CAN!
I'D LIKE THAT.

8. When are double-page splashes used in the book and why?

9. What is Rachel Carson's legacy? What is a legacy? Do you want a legacy? What makes a good legacy?

10. What do you think of the final panels of the book? What sort of feeling did they leave you with? Is there another way you think the book could or should have ended?

11. In general, this book focused on Rachel Carson's personal life as opposed to her achievements. How did that affect you as a reader? Do you feel it made you have more or less interest in Rachel's story?

8.

Post-Reading Activities

Reading:

1. In small groups, discuss the theme of birds throughout the book. Do they work as a theme? Pick one of the uses of the bird theme and explain to the class how it fits into the book and what its effect is on the reader.
2. Throughout the book, there are several suggestions of there being a gender division among scientists, that women and men working in scientific fields are treated differently. Find 3 examples in the book to support that statement. Do you think this division still exists today?
3. What do you think the author wants you to think or feel about Rachel Carson? Find examples of panels and text which support your opinion.

1.

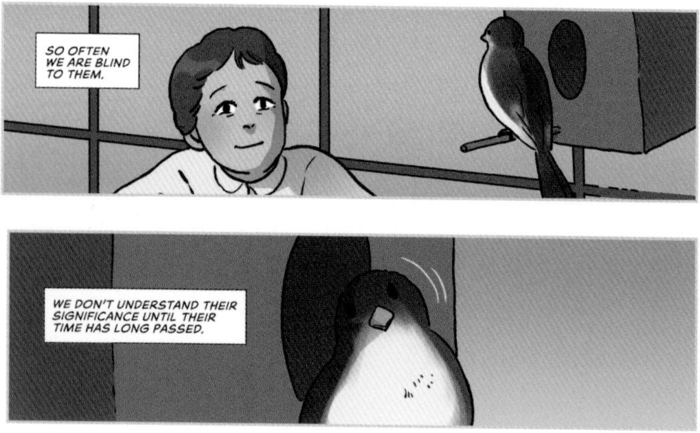
SO OFTEN WE ARE BLIND TO THEM.
WE DON'T UNDERSTAND THEIR SIGNIFICANCE UNTIL THEIR TIME HAS LONG PASSED.

Writing:

1. Rachel Carson had a lot of ups and downs in her life, and she accomplished many things. Write a newspaper article in which you interview Rachel on an element of her life that interests you.

2. Write a letter to Dorothy as Rachel during one of the following times, demonstrating how you think Rachel felt about her experiences:
   a. While she is sick
   b. When she decides to write *Silent Spring*
   c. After *Silent Spring* is published

3. Write a prose version of pages 14-15, 20-21, 24-25, or 32-33. What are some of the differences between prose and comic storytelling?

Speaking:

1. Break into groups and research the pros and cons of pesticide use. Have a class debate on whether there is a benefit to using pesticides.
2. On page 37, Rachel is heartbroken that those she believed were closest to her failed to understand her passion. What is your passion? Write a speech to convince others of the thing you're passionate about.

Why write about death when your work is so full of life?

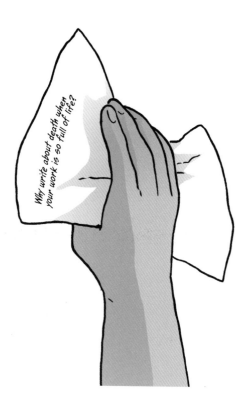

Integrating:

1. Research and write a biography of one of the other historical figures in the book (Marie Rodell, Paul Hermann Müller, or Dorothy Freeman).
2. Why do people sometimes ignore science or choose to eat foods that are bad for them? Research a healthy food or activity that you think people should choose more often, and create an ad explaining why they should. It can be a print ad, like you would see in a magazine, or a video ad, like a commercial.
3. "Can you imagine a perfect world?" (page 46) Rachel was driven by her passion to improve the world around her. What is your vision of a perfect world? Create a piece of art (visual arts, dance, music, creative writing) that conveys your vision. Include an artist's statement explaining your creative process and how your piece expresses your vision.

3.

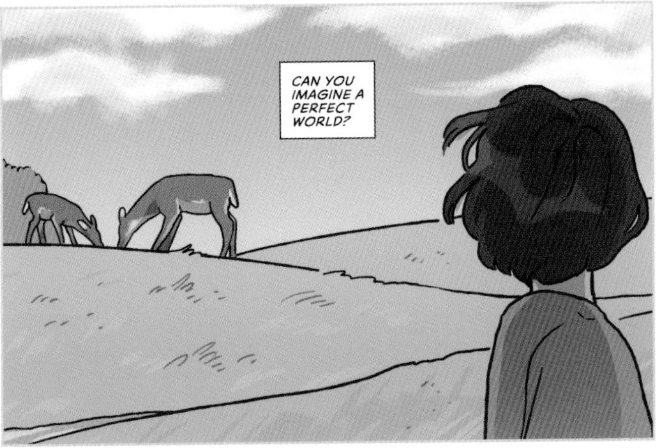
CAN YOU IMAGINE A PERFECT WORLD?

DISCOVER
ALL THE HITS

STEVENSON • ELLIS • WATTERS • ALLEN
LUMBERJANES
BEWARE THE KITTEN HOLY
NEW YORK TIMES BESTSELLING SERIES

Allison + Treiman + Cogar
GIANT DAYS
VOLUME ONE

RIBON • FISH • PEER
SLAM!
VOLUME ONE

Hope Larson • Brittney Williams • Sarah Stern
GOLDIE VANCE
Volume One

THE BACKSTAGERS

TYSON HESSE'S
DIESEL
IGNITION

BOOM! BOX™

AVAILABLE AT YOUR LOCAL COMICS SHOP AND BOOKSTORE
To find a comics shop in your area, visit www.comicshoplocator.com

WWW.**BOOM-STUDIOS**.COM

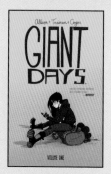

Lumberjanes
Noelle Stevenson, Shannon Watters, Grace Ellis, Brooklyn Allen, and Others
Volume 1: Beware the Kitten Holy
ISBN: 978-1-60886-687-8 | $14.99 US
Volume 2: Friendship to the Max
ISBN: 978-1-60886-737-0 | $14.99 US
Volume 3: A Terrible Plan
ISBN: 978-1-60886-803-2 | $14.99 US
Volume 4: Out of Time
ISBN: 978-1-60886-860-5 | $14.99 US
Volume 5: Band Together
ISBN: 978-1-60886-919-0 | $14.99 US

Giant Days
John Allison, Lissa Treiman, Max Sarin
Volume 1
ISBN: 978-1-60886-789-9 | $9.99 US
Volume 2
ISBN: 978-1-60886-804-9 | $14.99 US
Volume 3
ISBN: 978-1-60886-851-3 | $14.99 US

Jonesy
Sam Humphries, Caitlin Rose Boyle
Volume 1
ISBN: 978-1-60886-883-4 | $9.99 US
Volume 2
ISBN: 978-1-60886-999-2 | $14.99 US

Slam!
Pamela Ribon, Veronica Fish, Brittany Peer
Volume 1
ISBN: 978-1-68415-004-5 | $14.99 US

Goldie Vance
Hope Larson, Brittney Williams
Volume 1
ISBN: 978-1-60886-898-8 | $9.99 US
Volume 2
ISBN: 978-1-60886-974-9 | $14.99 US

The Backstagers
James Tynion IV, Rian Sygh
Volume 1
ISBN: 978-1-60886-993-0 | $14.99 US

Tyson Hesse's Diesel: Ignition
Tyson Hesse
ISBN: 978-1-60886-907-7 | $14.99 US

Coady & The Creepies
Liz Prince, Amanda Kirk, Hannah Fisher
ISBN: 978-1-68415-029-8 | $14.99 US